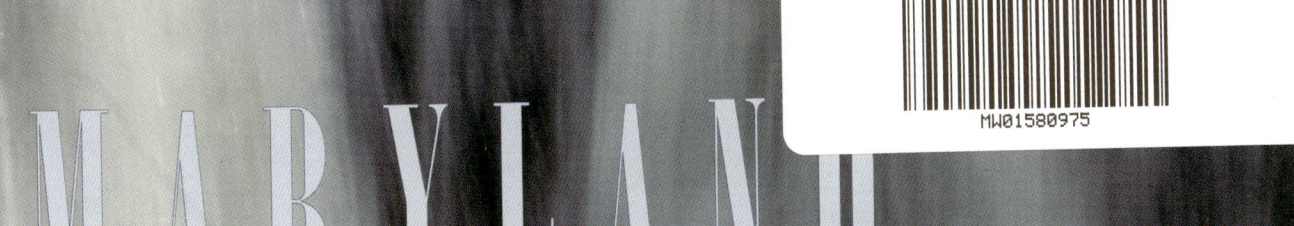

MARYLAND
Wonder and Light

PHOTOGRAPHY BY
IAN J. PLANT

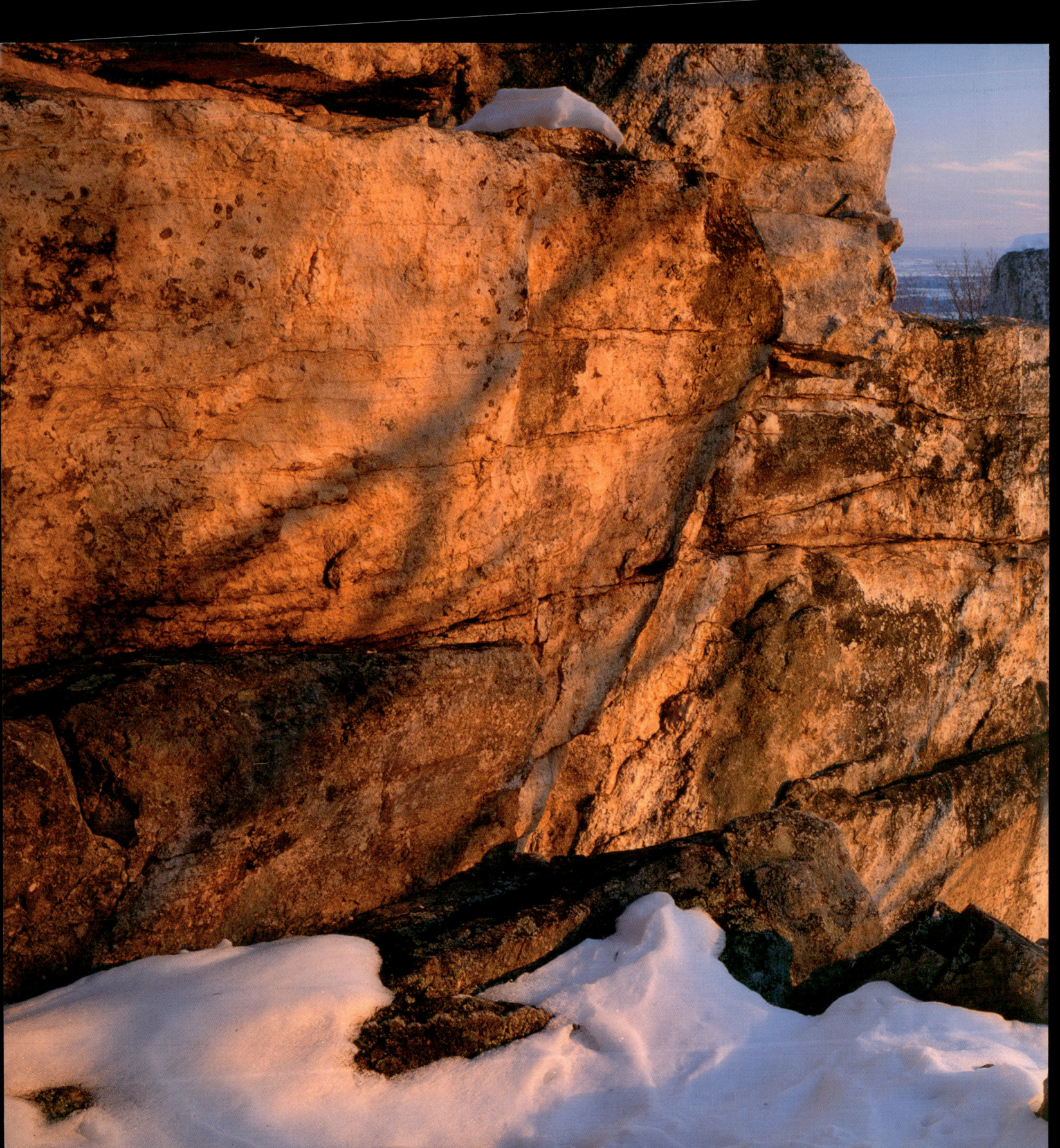

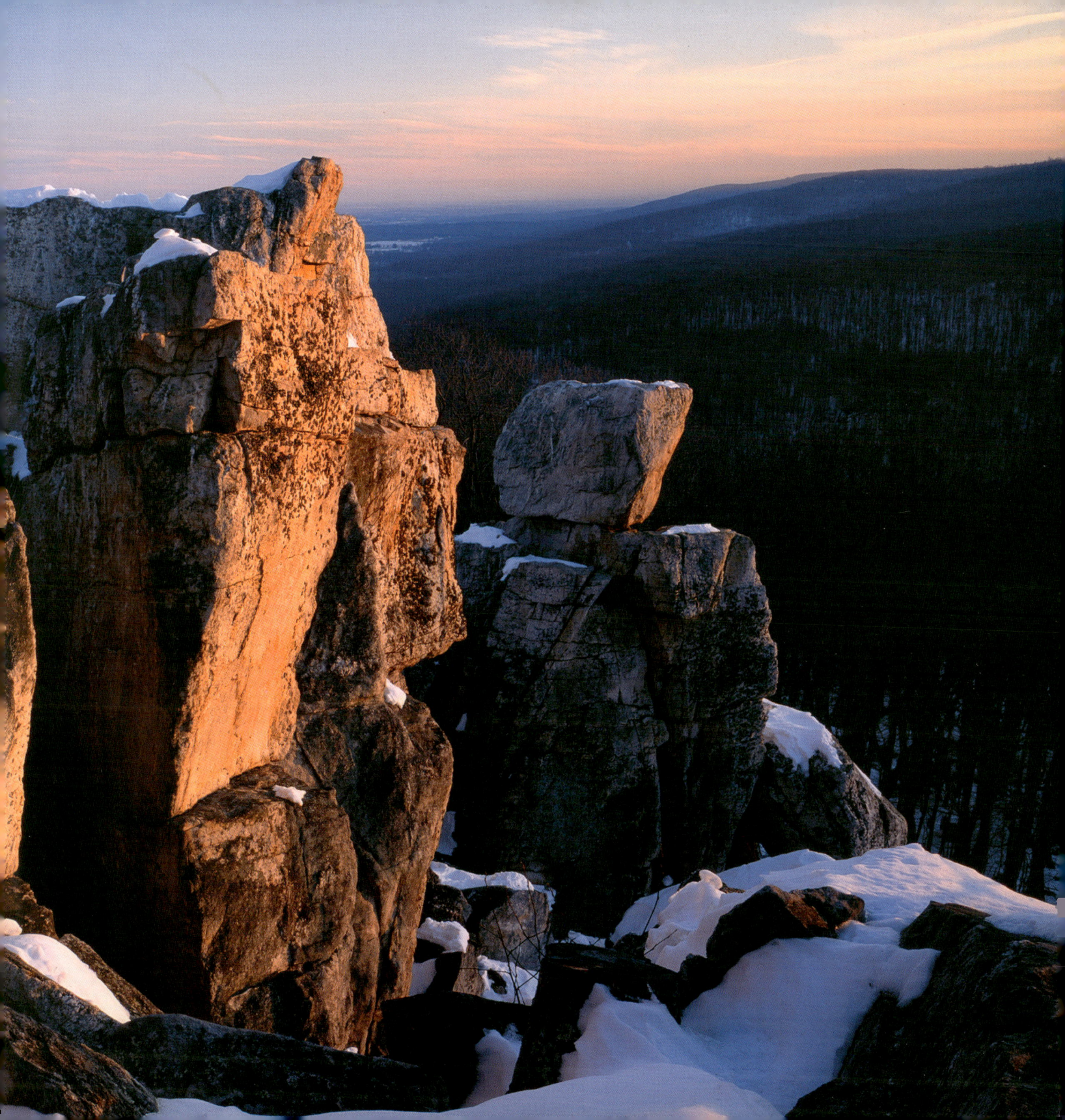

MARYLAND
WONDER AND LIGHT

Photography by
Ian J. Plant

Mountain Trail Press

1818 Presswood Road • Johnson City, Tennessee 37604
www.mountaintrailpress.com

Celebrating America's Most Scenic Places

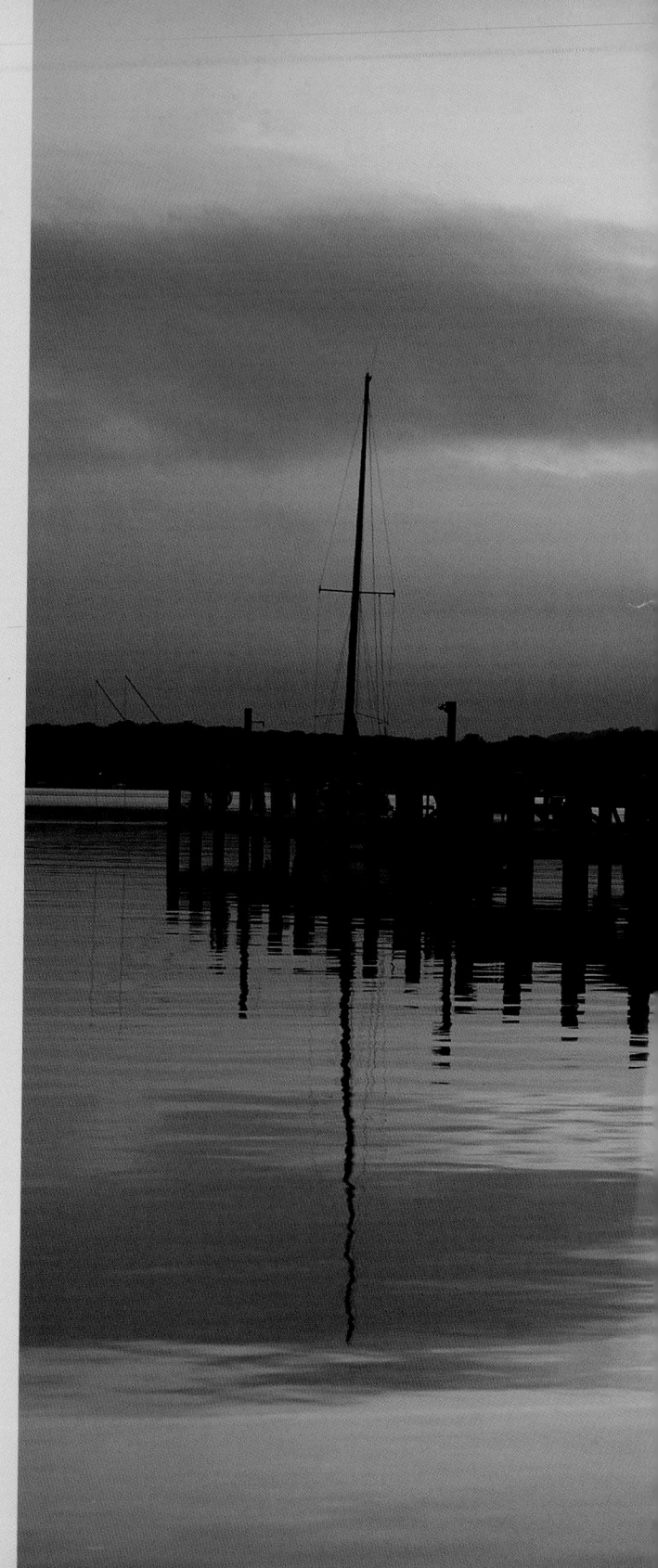

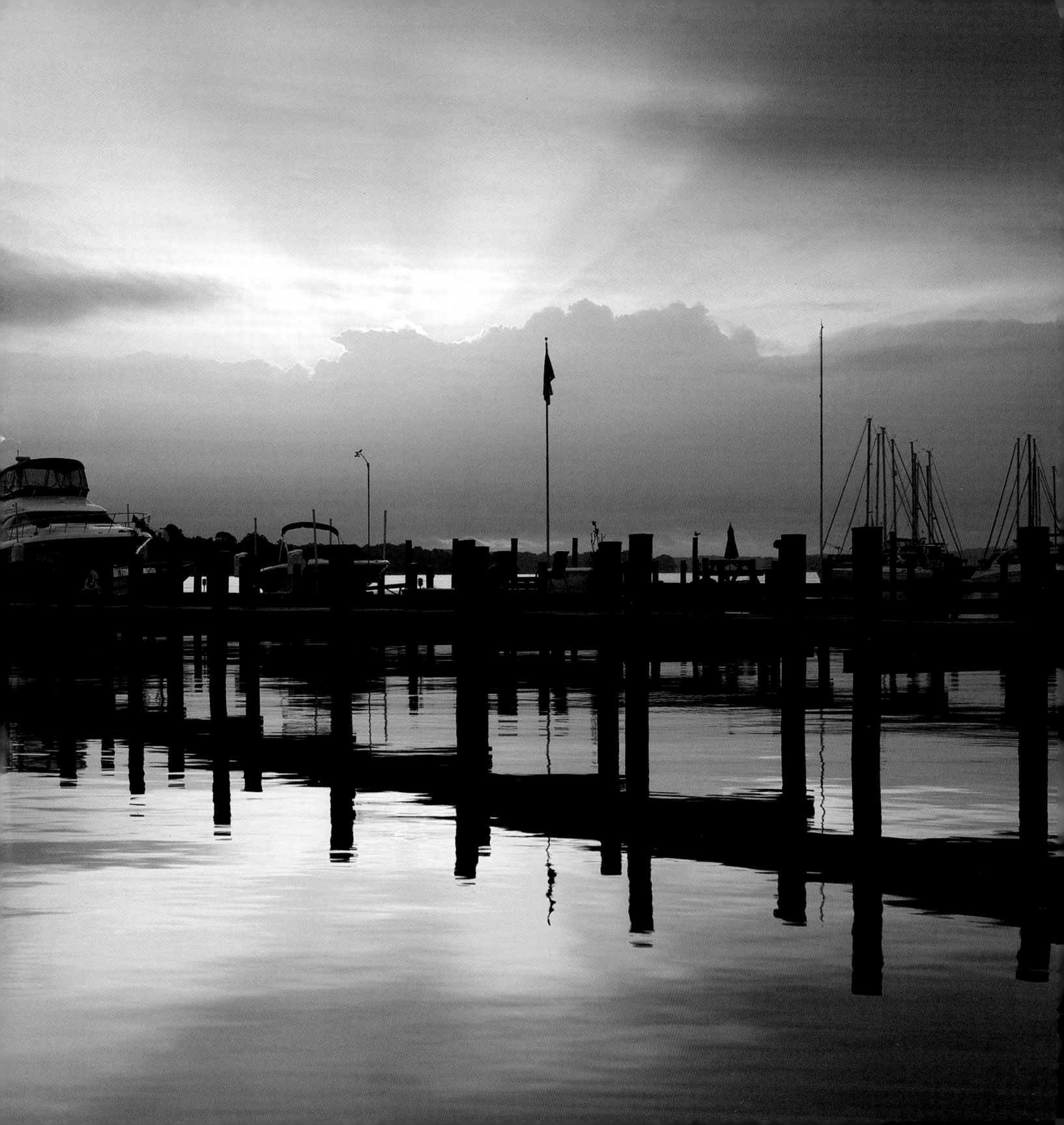

MARYLAND
Wonder and Light

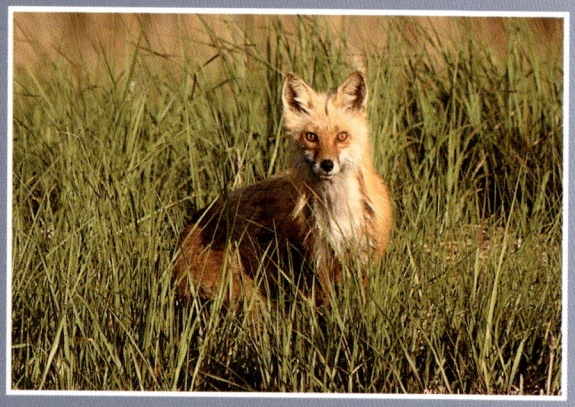

IAN J. PLANT

Book design: Ian J. Plant
Editor: Jerry D. Greer

Published by Mountain Trail Press LLC
1818 Presswood Road
Johnson City, TN 37604

ISBN: 0-9777933-0-3
Printed in Korea
First Printing, Fall 2006

Front cover: Sunrise over the Atlantic Ocean, Assateague Island National Seashore.

First frontispiece: A great blue heron pauses beneath Great Falls of the Potomac.

Full page spread: Chimney Rocks in winter, Catoctin Mountain Park.

Preceding page: Sunrise over Magothy Harbor on the Chesapeake Bay.

Right: Crescent moon and sunset clouds, Patapsco Valley State Park.

Above: A curious red fox roams Barren Island, located on the Eastern Shore of the Chesapeake Bay.

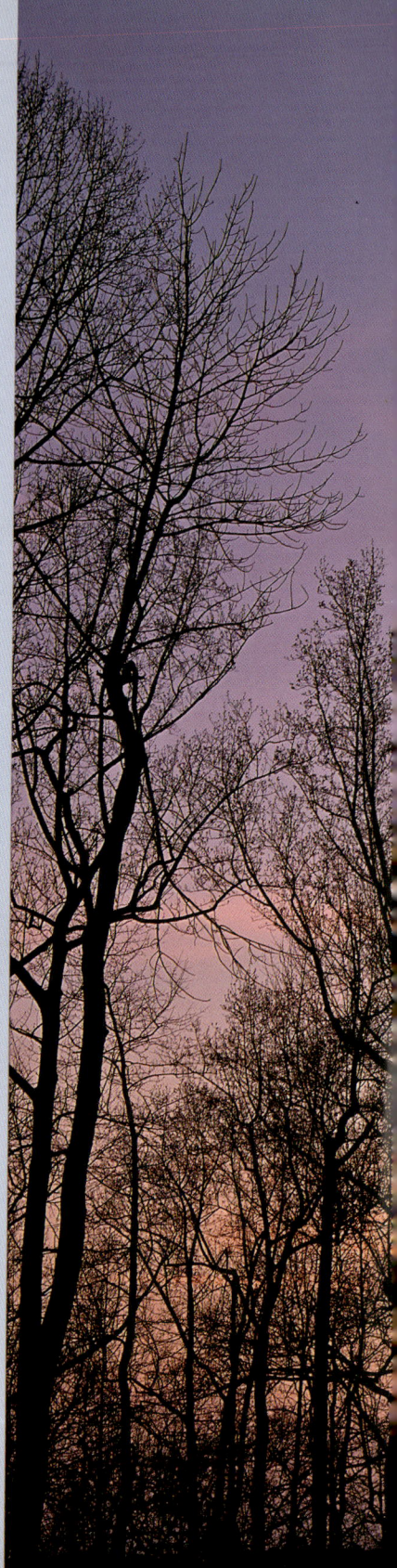

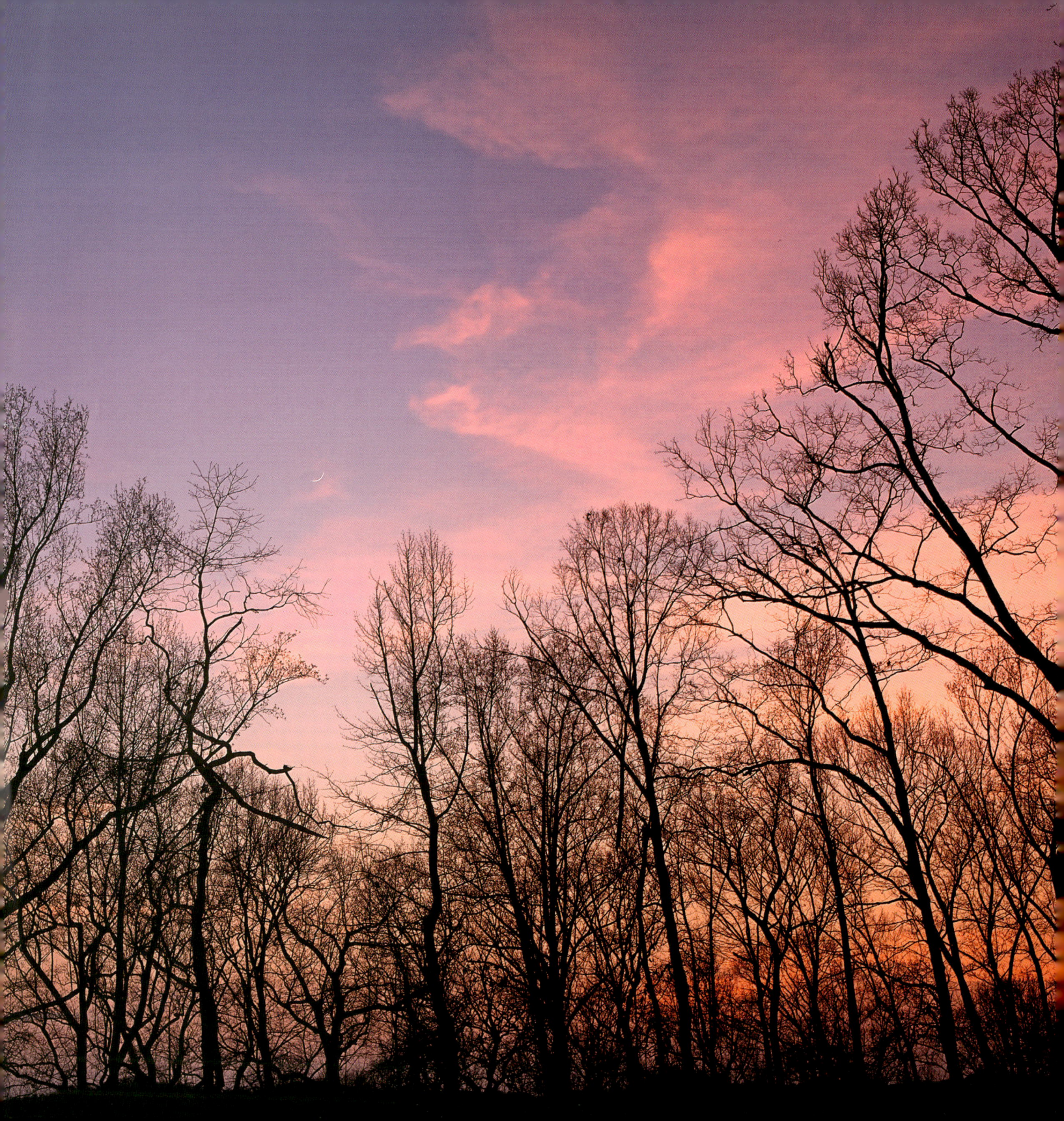

*M*ARYLAND is a state of surprising beauty. Maryland has been called "America in Miniature" because so much is packed into this small state. Just about every natural feature can be found here - mountains, cliffs, waterfalls, marsh, bay, and ocean. And although technically not desert, the sandy shores and windswept dunes of the Atlantic coast nonetheless echo, if only in a small way, the great deserts of the American West. Maryland also has its own unique natural beauty, found nowhere else in the world.

Humans first came to the area more than 10,000 years ago from other parts of North America. By the time Europeans arrived, many different Native American tribes called the land now known as Maryland home. Their imprint on the land is most clearly seen from the names of many of Maryland's special places – such as Chesapeake, Potomac, Piscataway, Mattowoman, Accokeek, and Choptank – names that serve as a reminder of these flourishing indigenous societies.

Maryland is defined by the tension between land and water. To the west, the Appalachian Mountains march through the state, leaving their indelible mark. Steep rocky mountains characterize this landscape. To the east, Maryland is dominated by the

Chesapeake Bay – one of the world's greatest estuaries, a magical place where fresh and salt waters mix – and the restless shores of the Atlantic Ocean.

Connecting these two worlds is the mighty Potomac River. The transition between mountain and sea occurs along the fall line, which begins at Great Falls. The transition is a spectacular one; the River suddenly narrows and drops 76 feet over cascades and waterfalls, and then travels for several miles through Mather Gorge, with cliffs rising 100 feet above the water. The sheer volume of water flowing through the Gorge is phenomenal, and at times overflows the cliffs themselves. The fall line ends at Little Falls, where the Potomac ceases to be powered by gravity, and instead becomes part of the ocean, powered by tides and wind.

Within these three worlds – mountains, river, and sea – Maryland plays host to some of the most diverse wildlife in the United States. Ranging from the majestic bald eagle to the wild ponies of Assateague Island, Maryland is home to many species, some found nowhere else on Earth. As long as Maryland's wild places stay wild, "America in Miniature" will continue to support a diversity of flora and fauna that make Maryland truly one of America's most unique and special places.

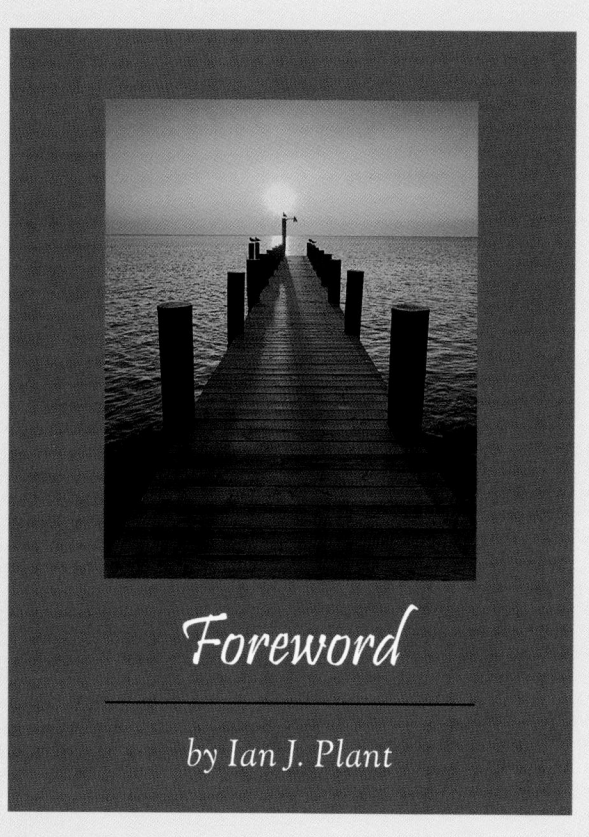

Foreword

by Ian J. Plant

The rising sun spreads rays of light over a dock on Tilghman Island, located on Maryland's famous Eastern Shore.

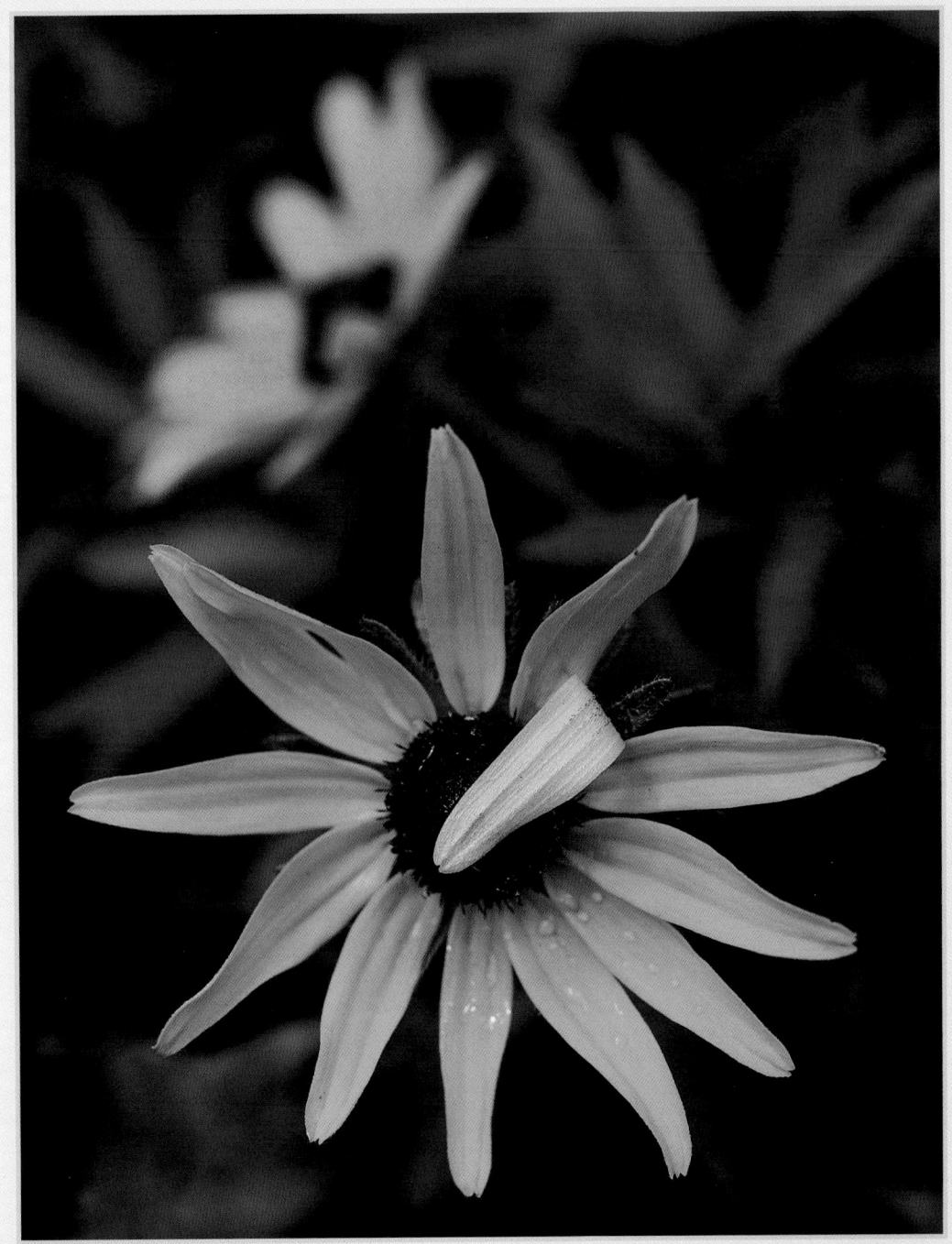

Black-eyed susan, the state flower of Maryland.

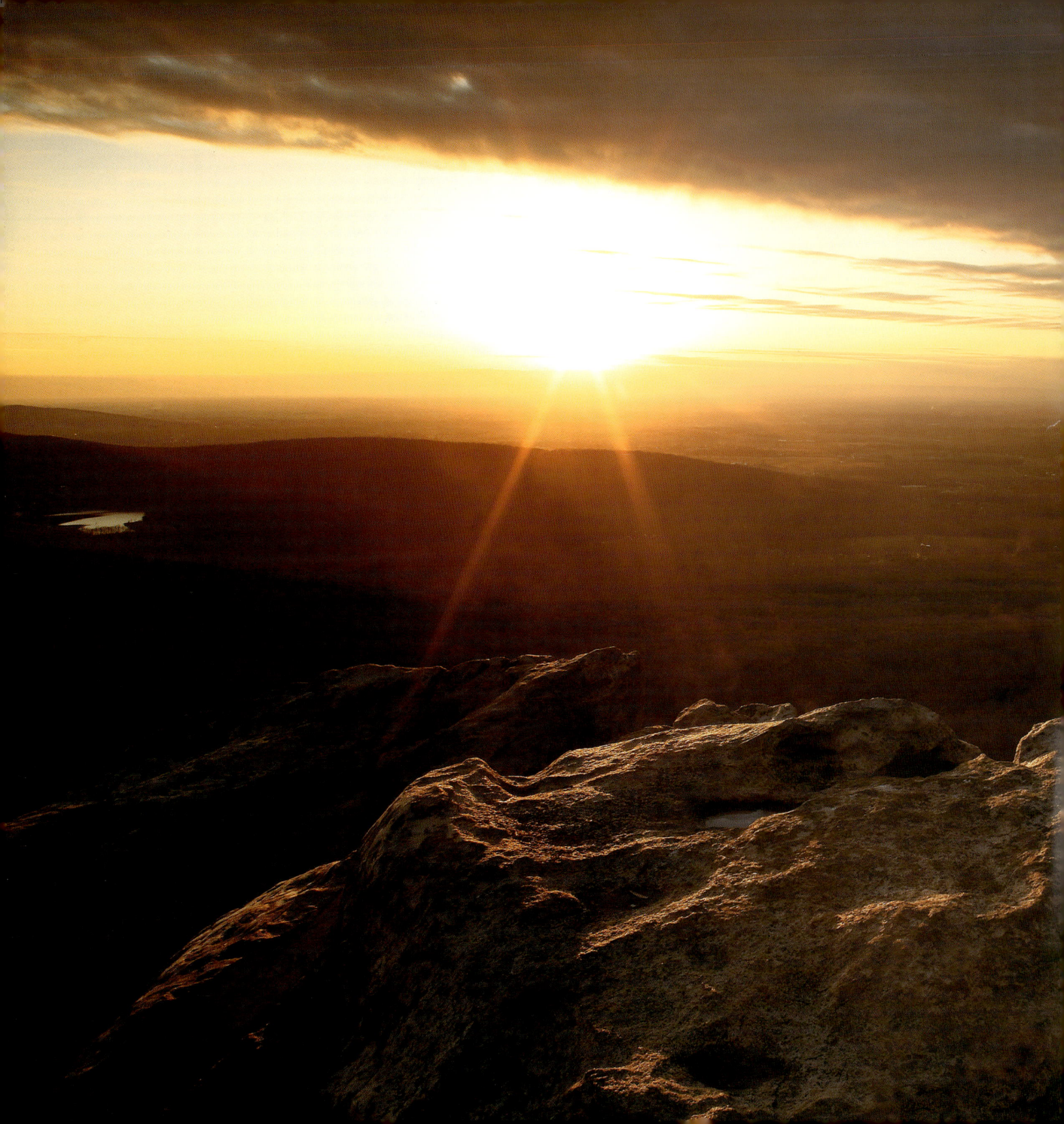

VIEW FROM ANNAPOLIS ROCKS, along the Appalachian Trail. The world-renowned Trail, which stretches from Georgia to Maine, passes through Maryland for nearly 40 miles. Annapolis Rocks, a favorite destination of locals and thru-hikers alike, offers spectacular views of Greenbrier Lake and the Cumberland Valley to the west.

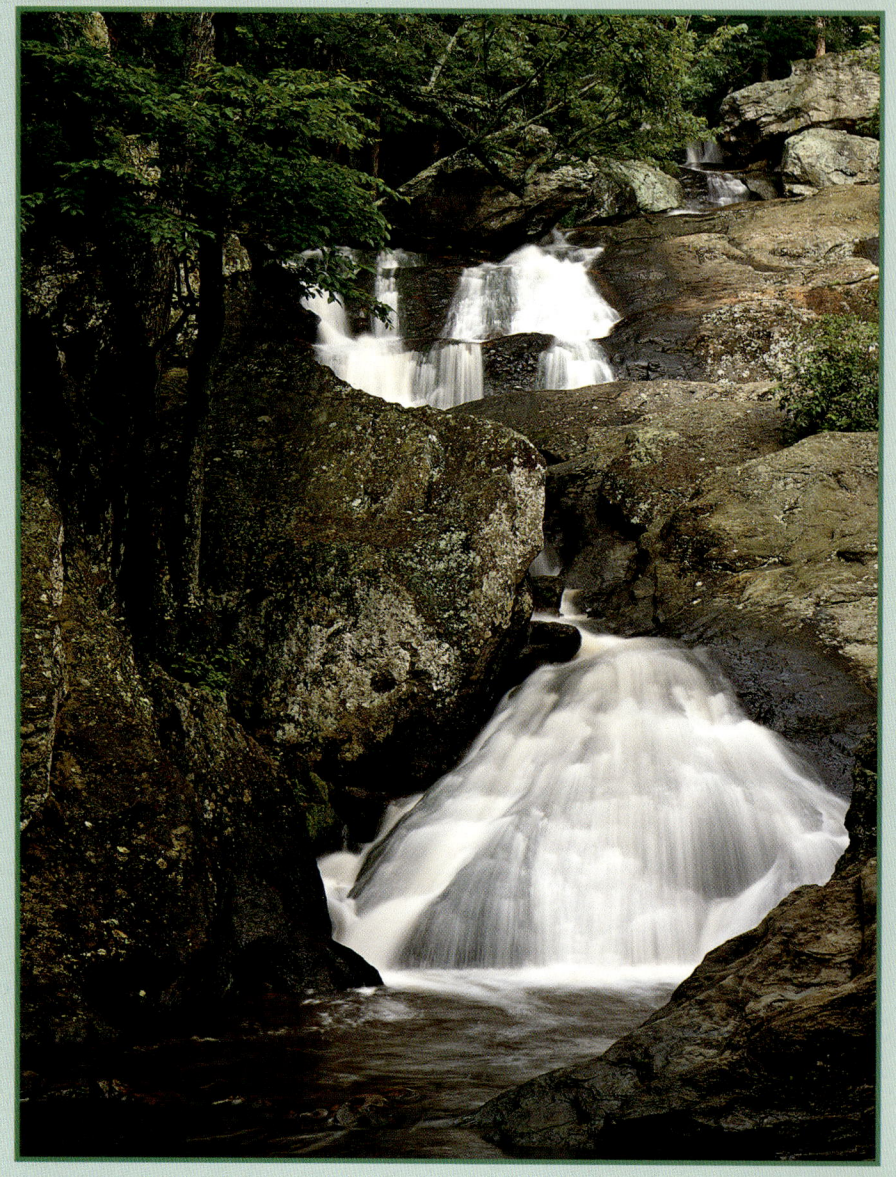

Above: Cunningham Falls, located in the Catoctin Mountains, cascades 78 feet over boulders and cliffs.

Right: A snowy egret shakes itself dry after plunging into a tidal pool.

Next page: Fall color and sunset light seen from Dan's Rock, overlooking the mountains and valleys of Allegany County.

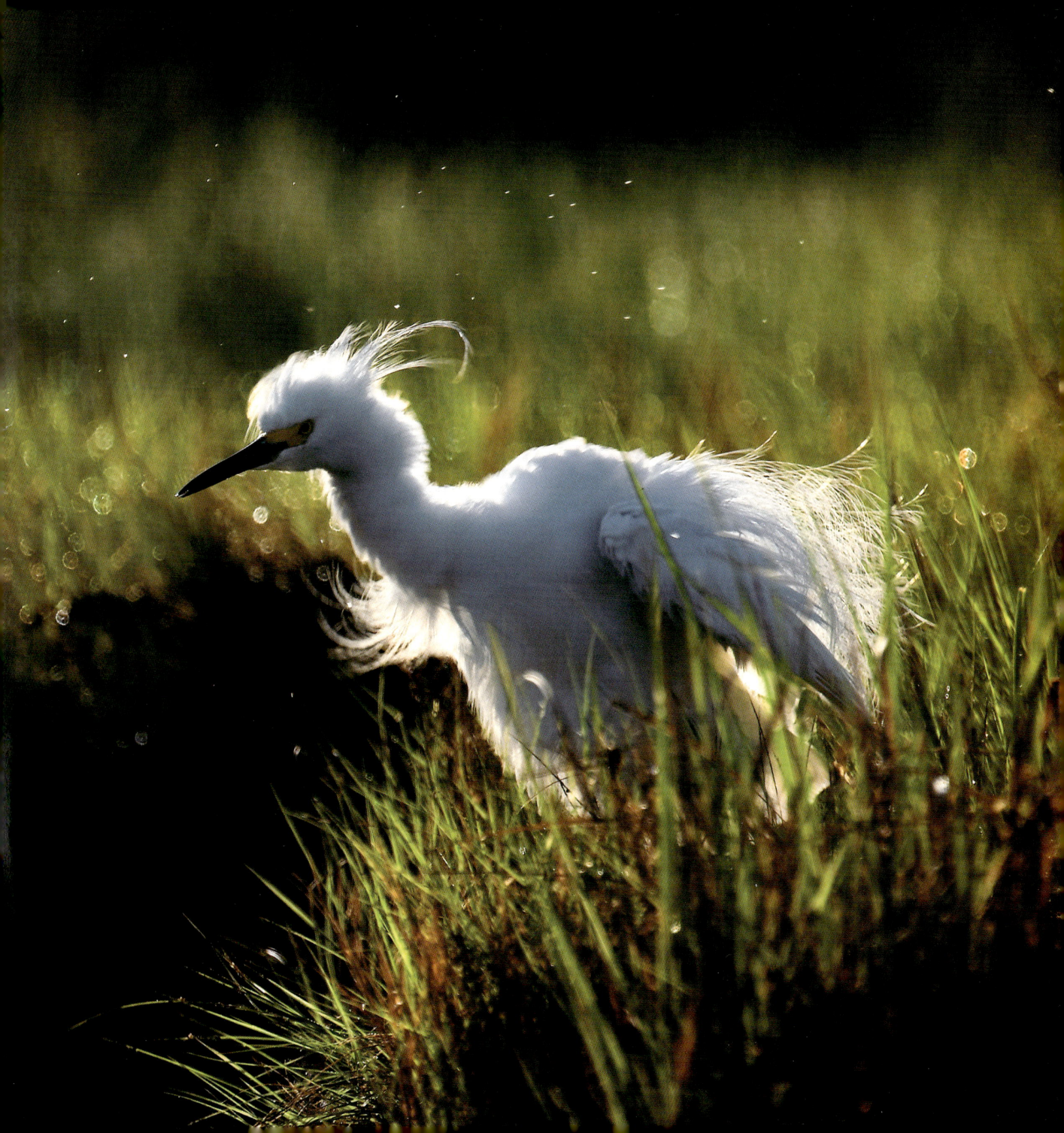

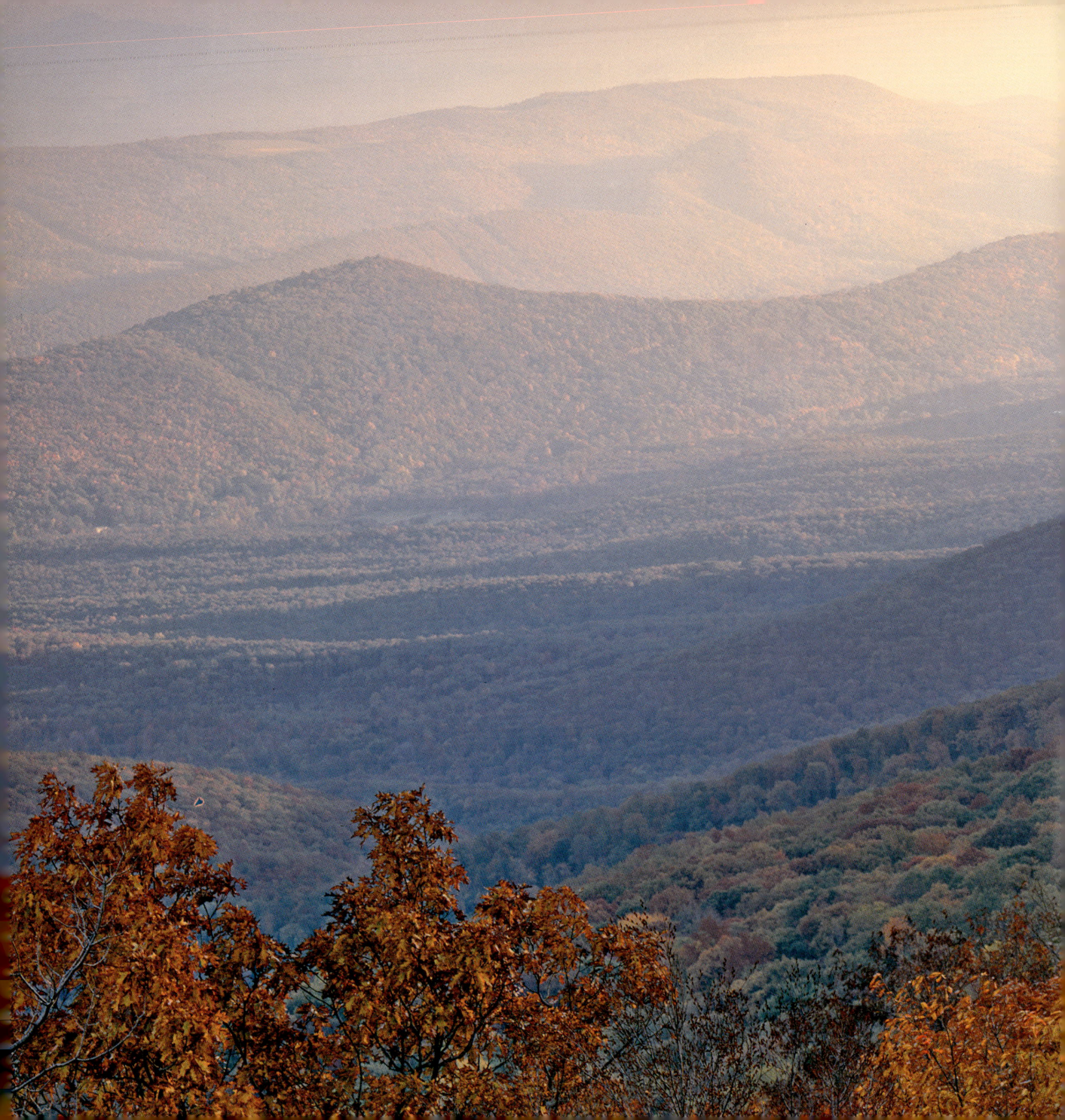

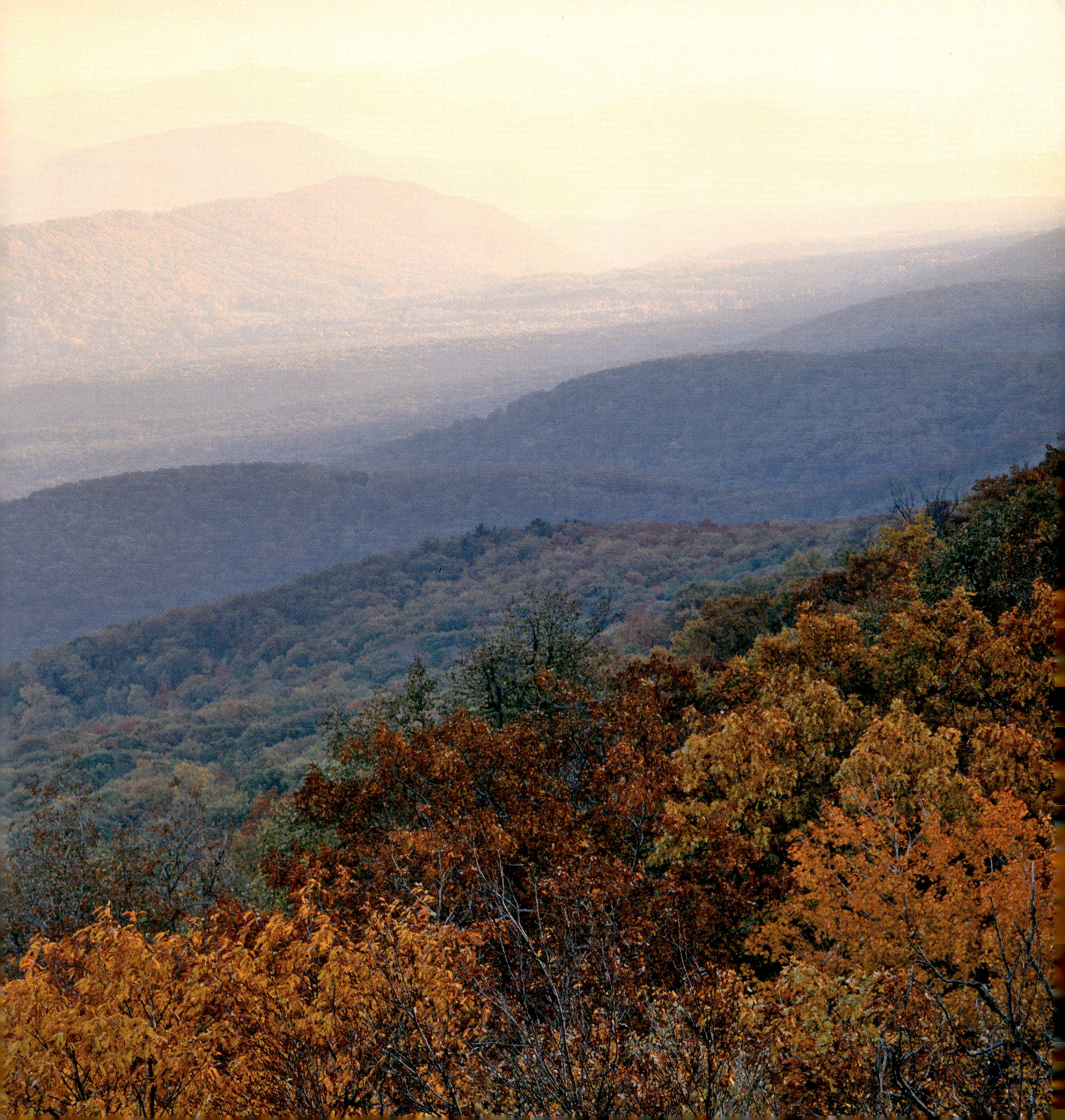

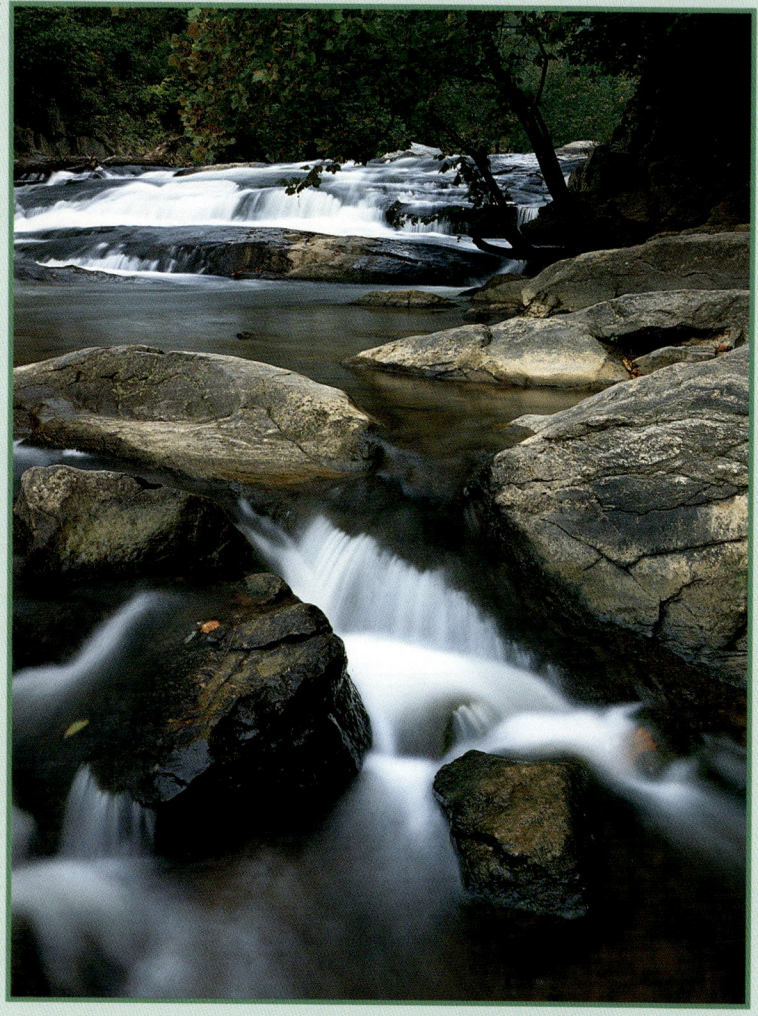

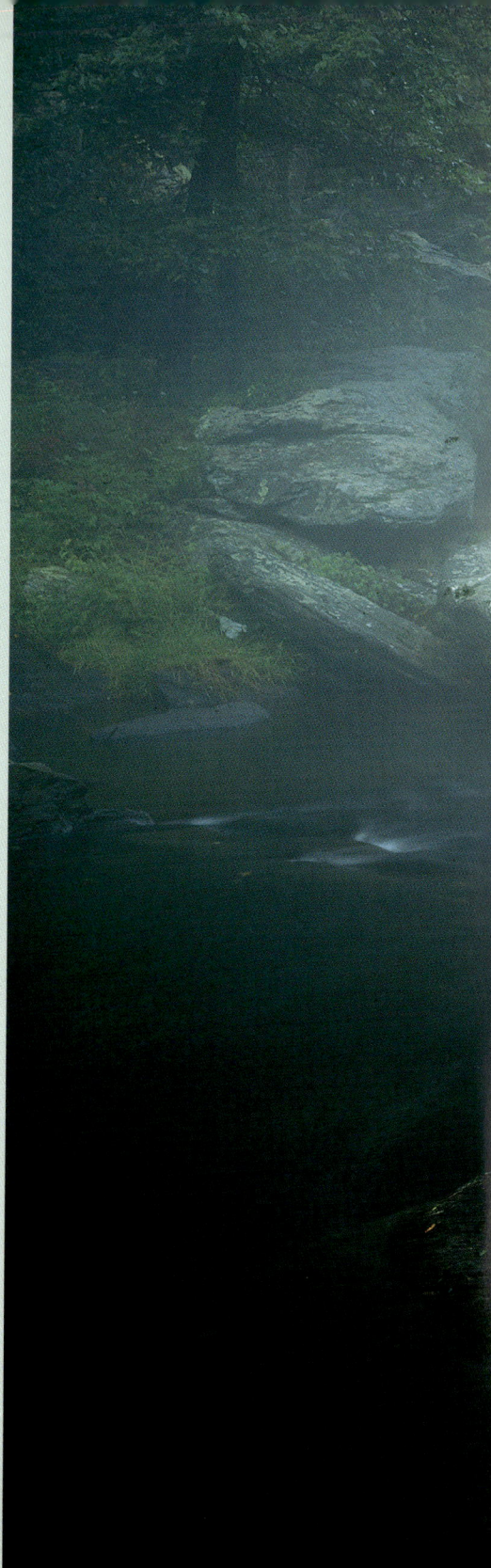

Above: The McKeldin Rapids, Patapsco River State Park.

Right: Fog along Big Gunpowder Falls. The "Falls" in the name refers to the stream passing over the fall line which separates the piedmont from the coastal plain.

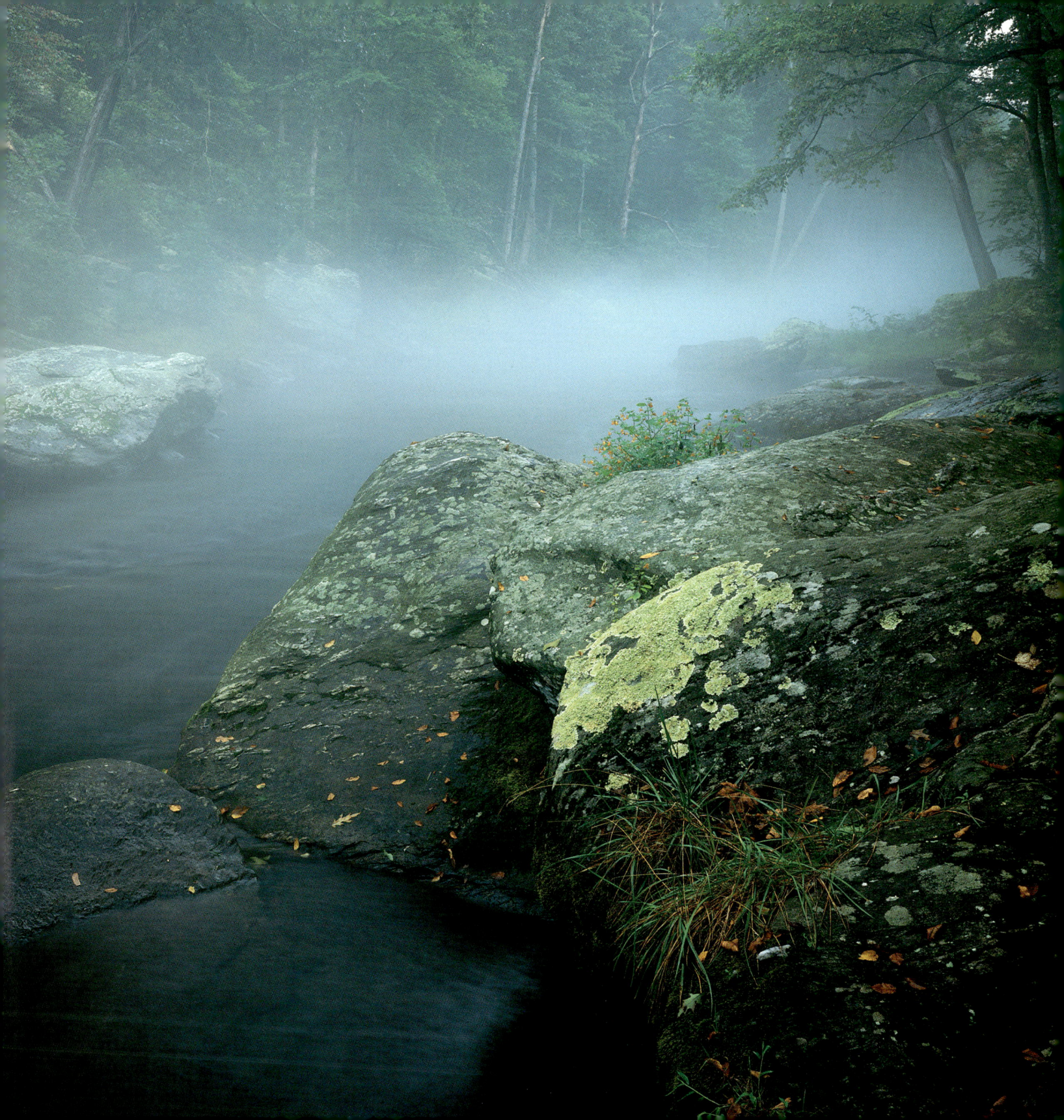

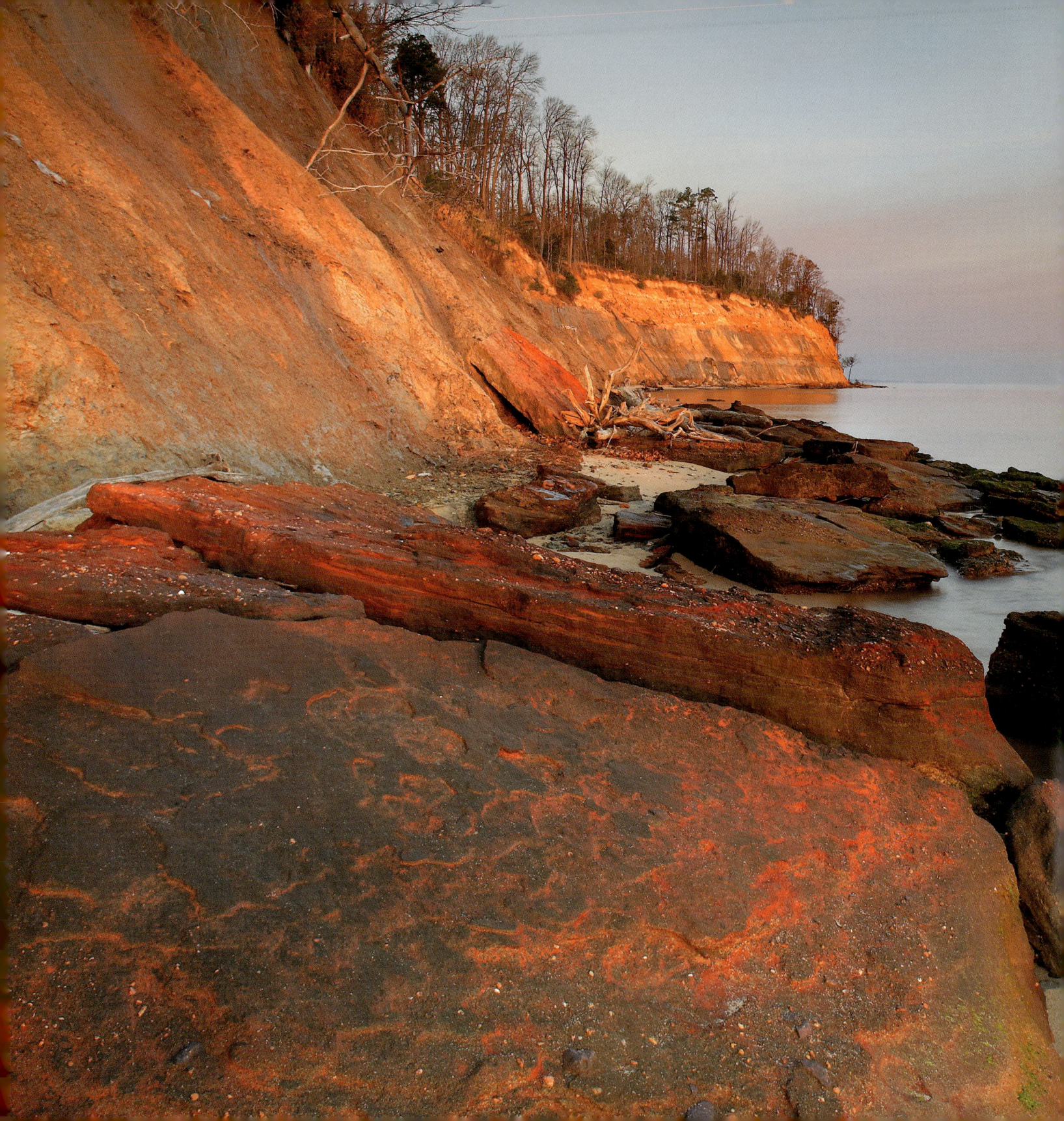

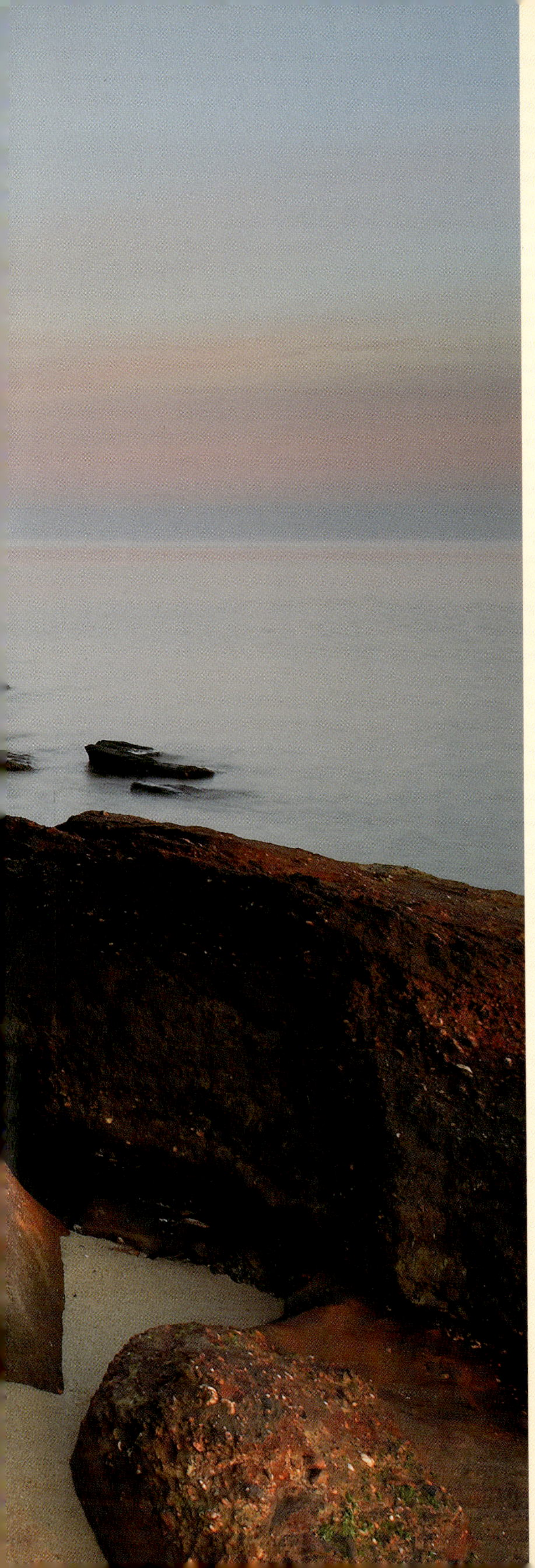

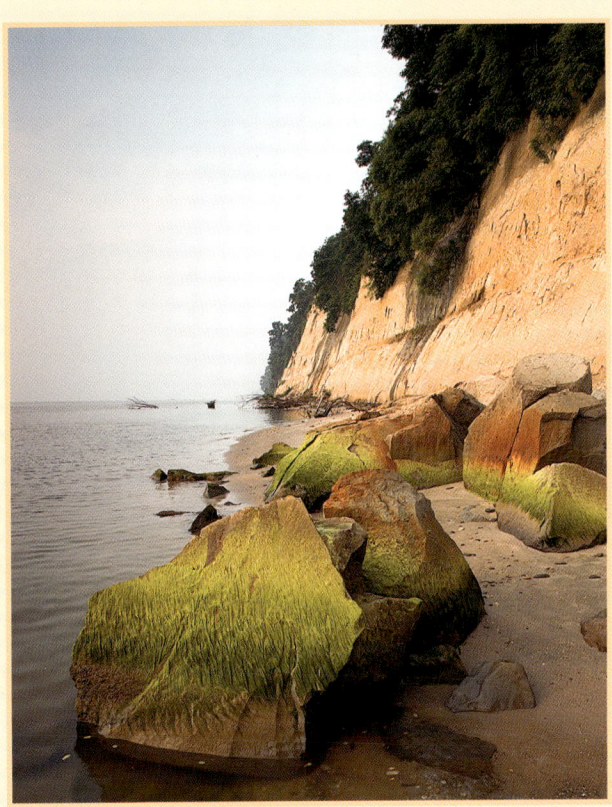

THE CALVERT CLIFFS stretch for 40 miles on Maryland's Western Shore of the Chesapeake Bay from Chesapeake Beach to Drum Point. Formed over 15 million years ago when all of southern Maryland was covered by a warm, shallow sea, over 600 species of fossils have been identified from these cliffs, with the teeth of various species of shark being the most abundant. Primarily made of layers of soft clay, close observation reveals the cliffs to be a kaleidoscope of pastel blues, yellows, oranges, purples, and reds – with a splash of brilliant greens added where seaweed has gained a foothold on the rocks.

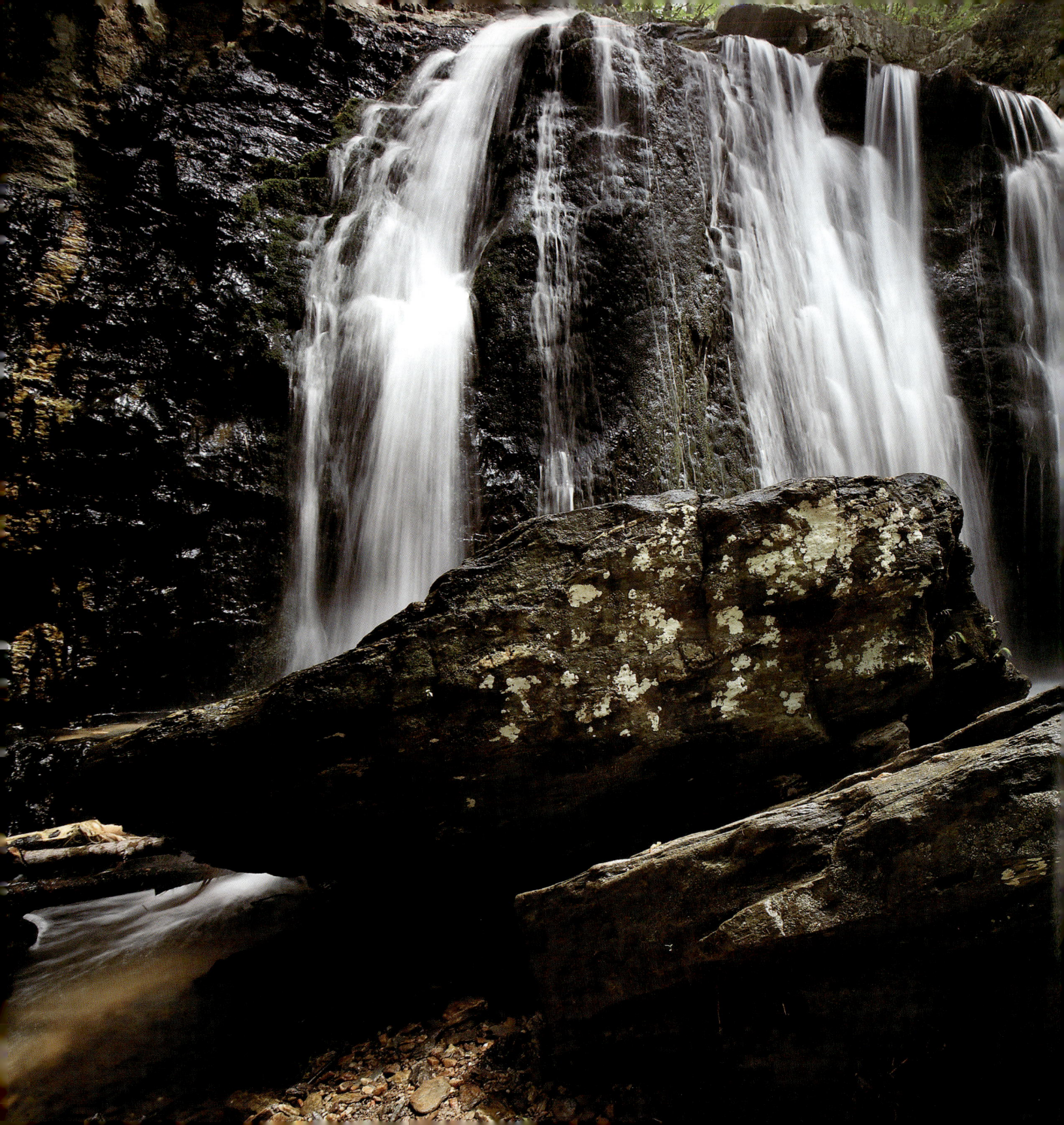

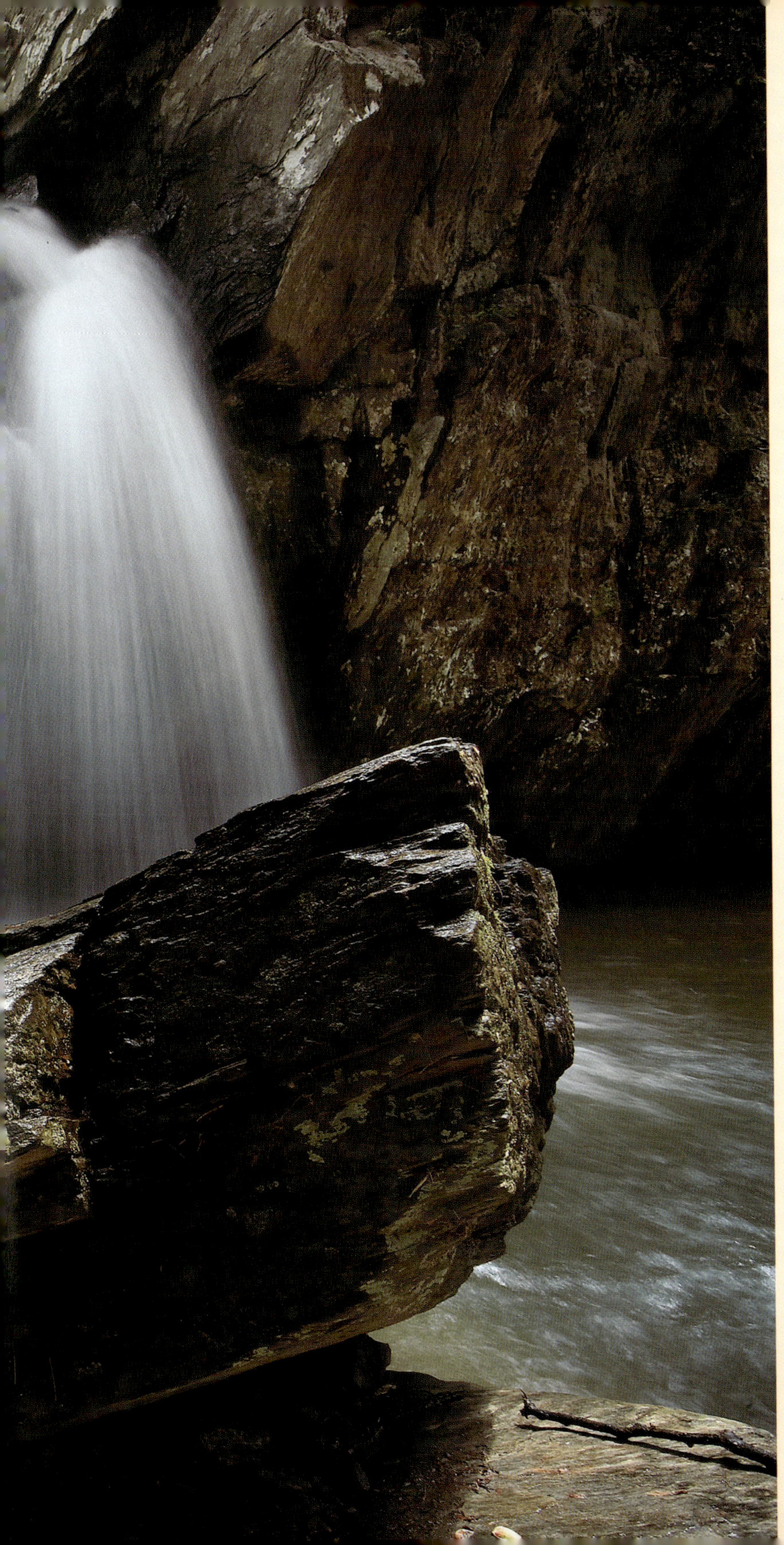

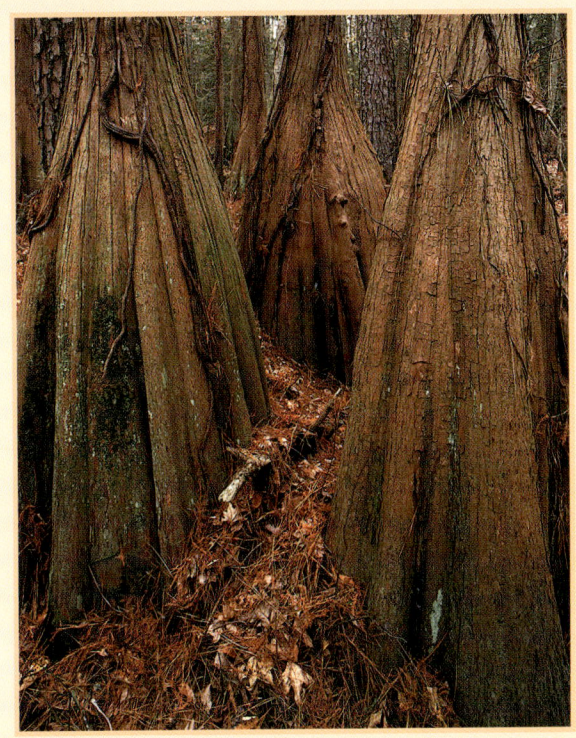

Left: Kilgore Falls, located in the Falling Branch Area of Rocks State Park, just north of Baltimore.

Above: Bald cypress trees are abundant along Corker's Creek, part of Pocomoke River State Park on the Eastern Shore.

Next page: Sunrise breaks through morning mist on the lonely shores of James Island, located on the Chesapeake Bay. James Island, like many islands on the Chesapeake, is slowly disappearing because of rising sea levels and erosion.

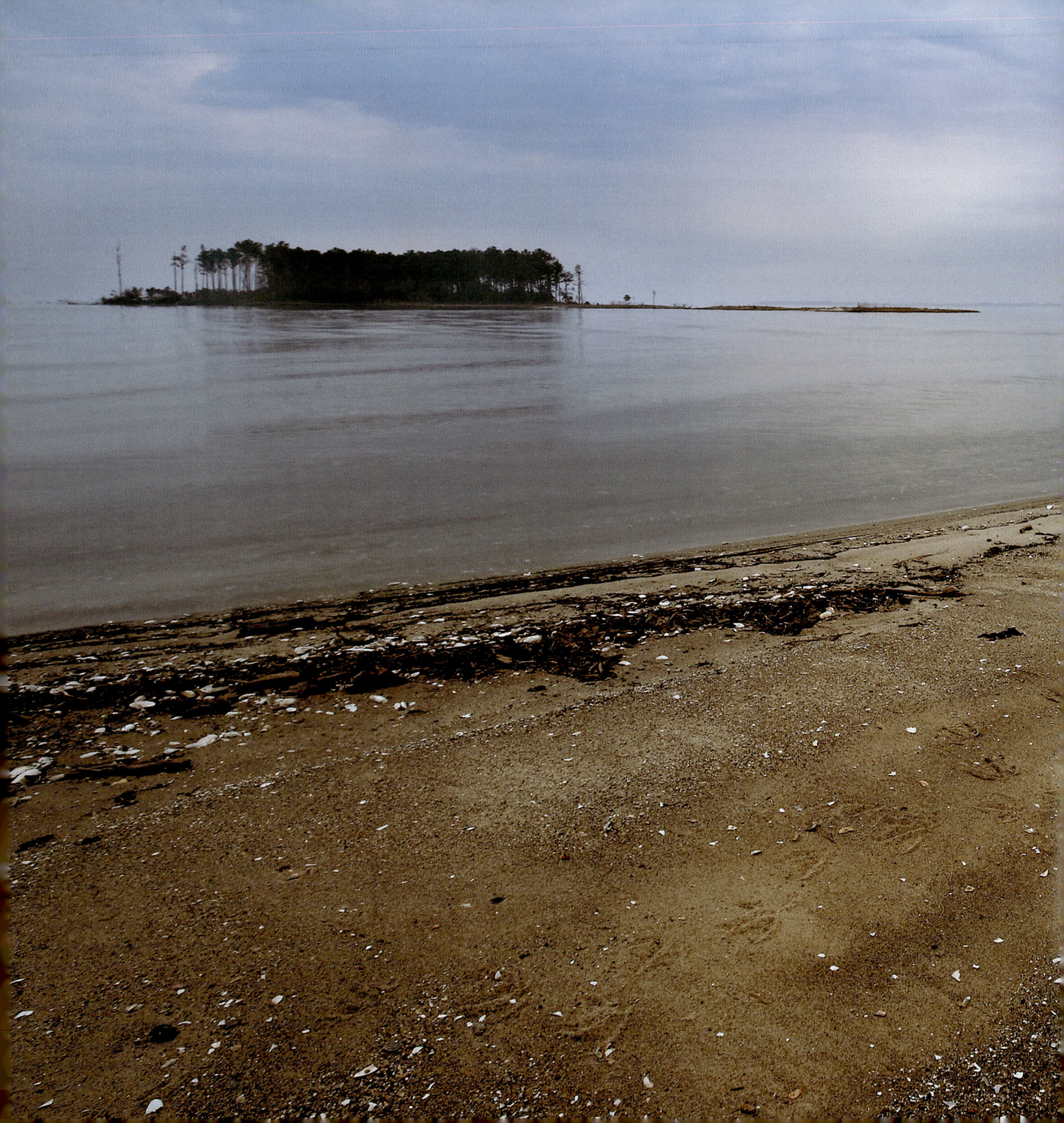

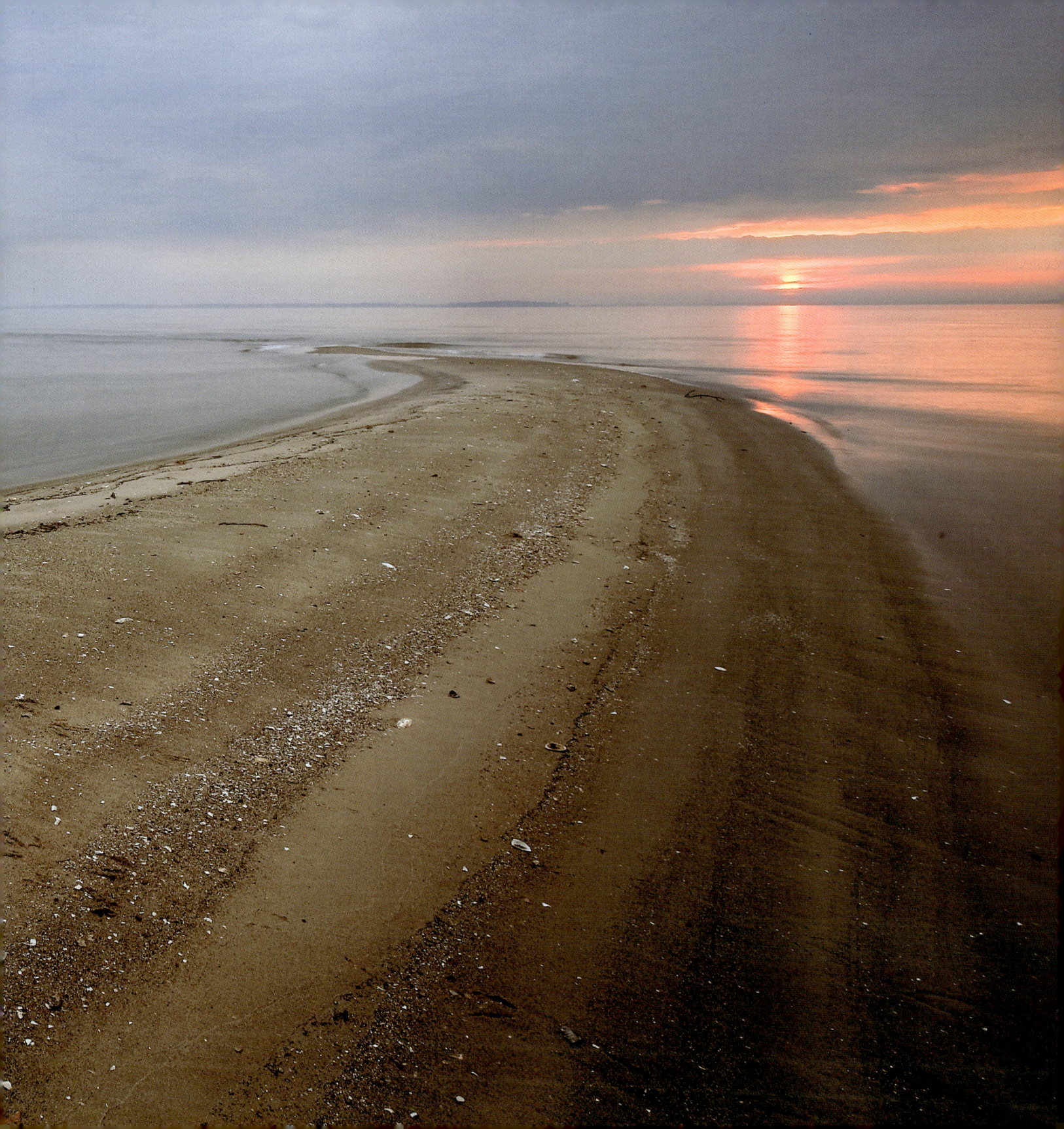

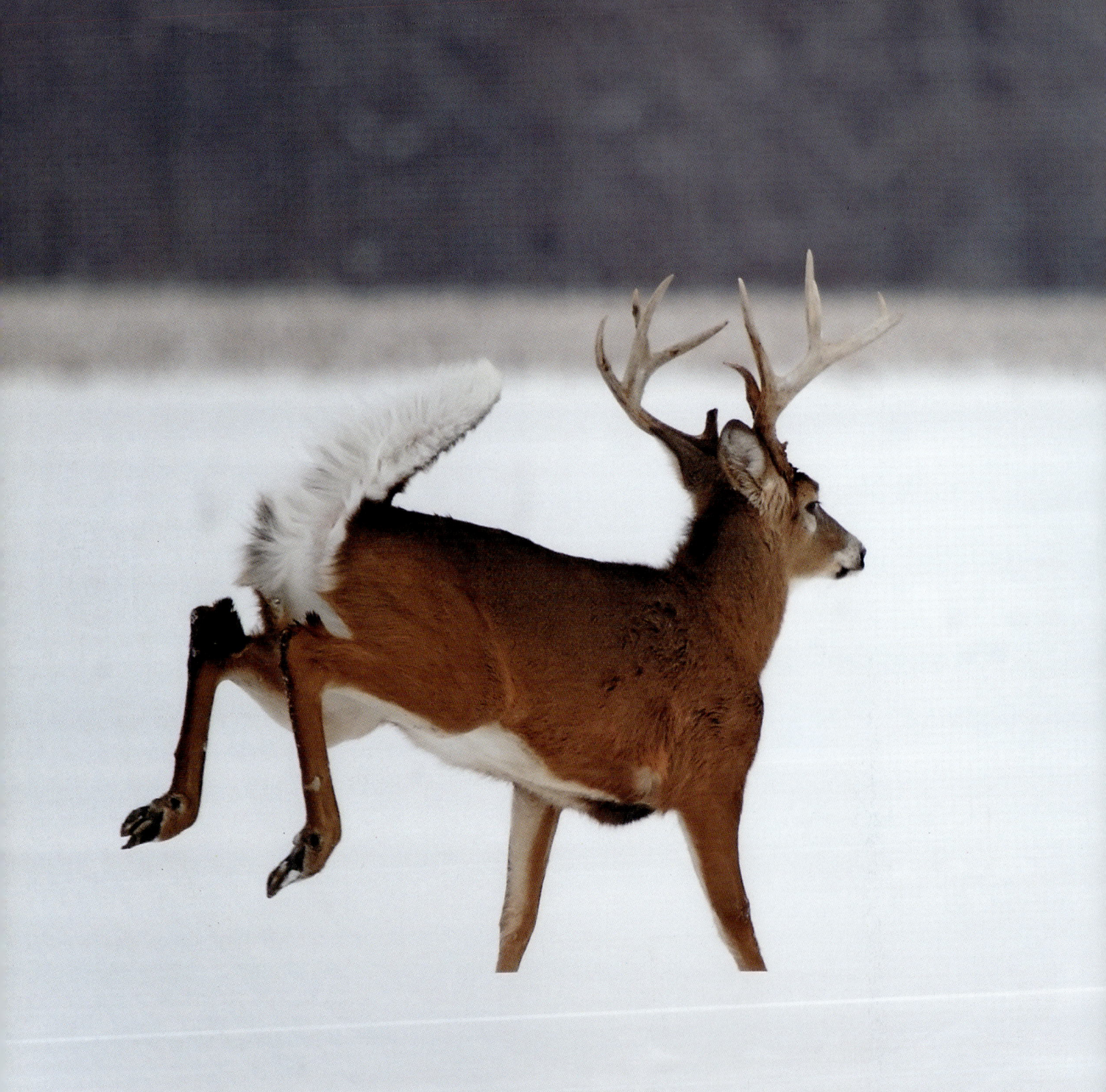

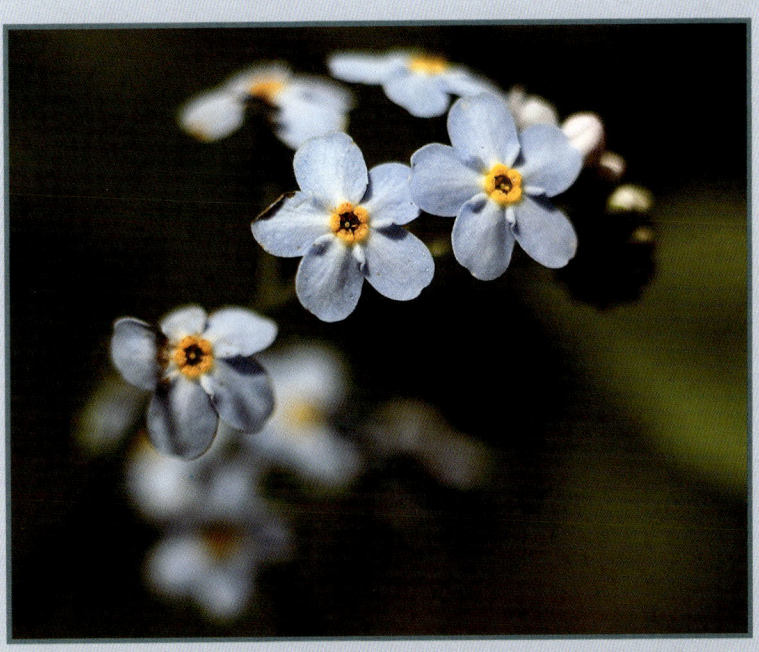

Left: A white-tailed deer buck sprints for safety on Wye Island, located on the Eastern Shore.

Above: Bluets bloom in spring at Rocks State Park.

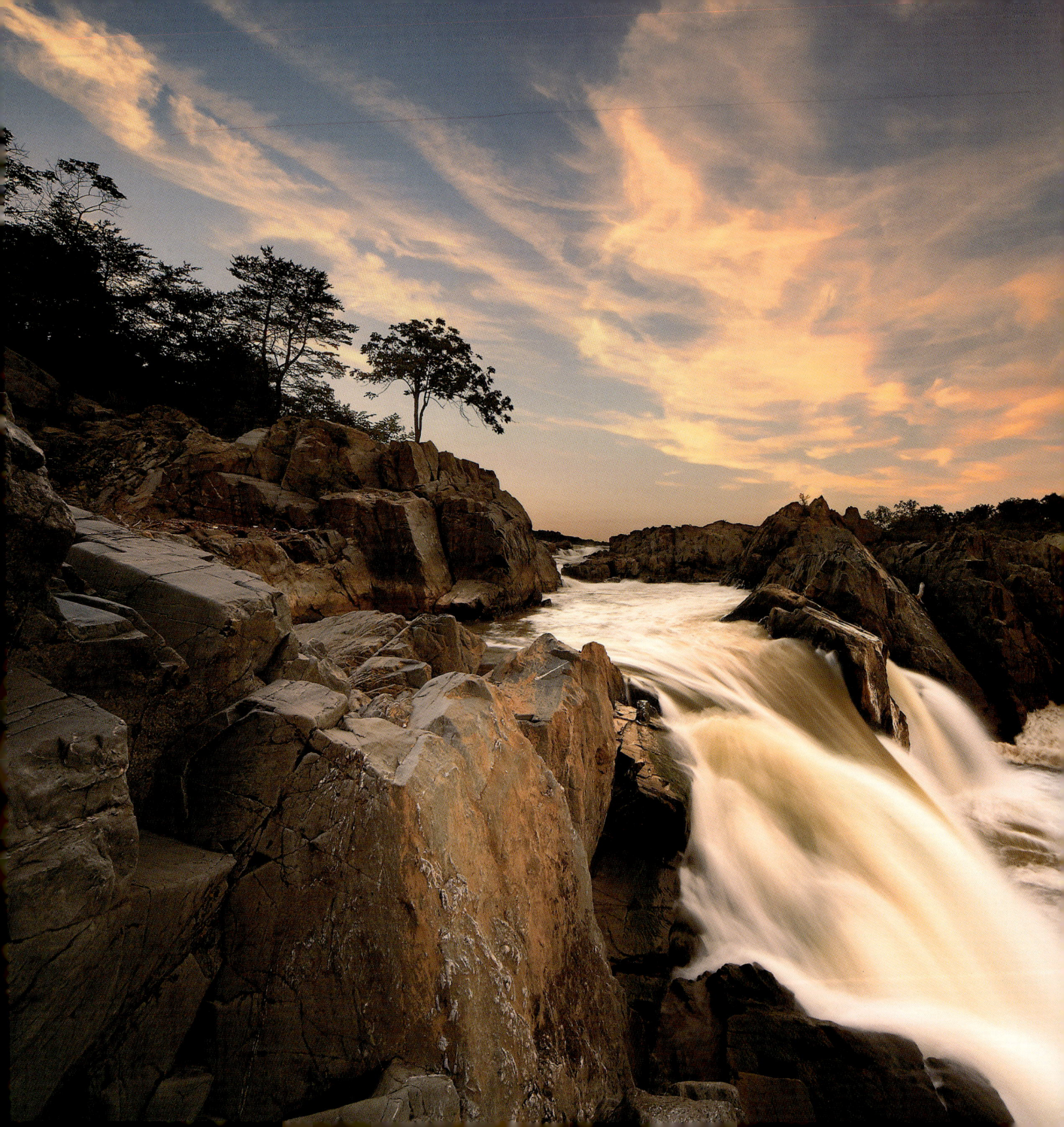

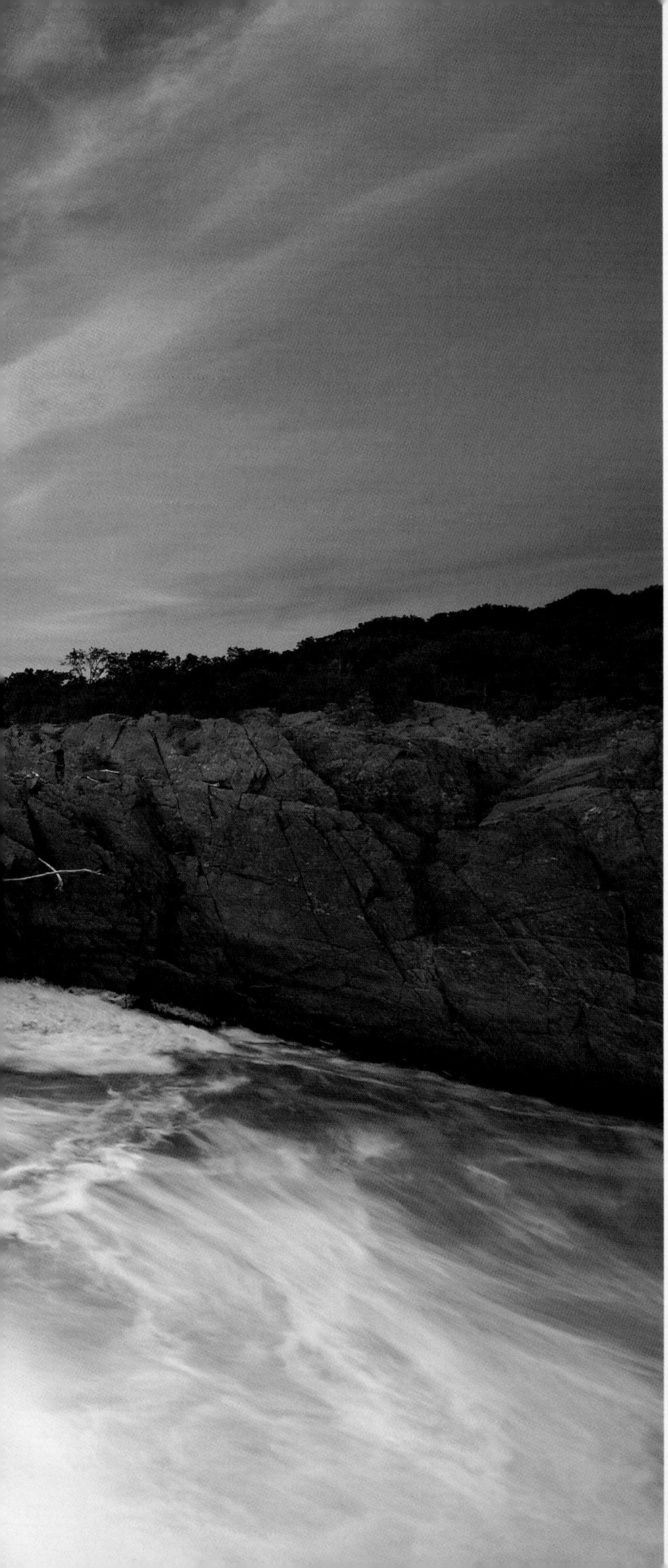

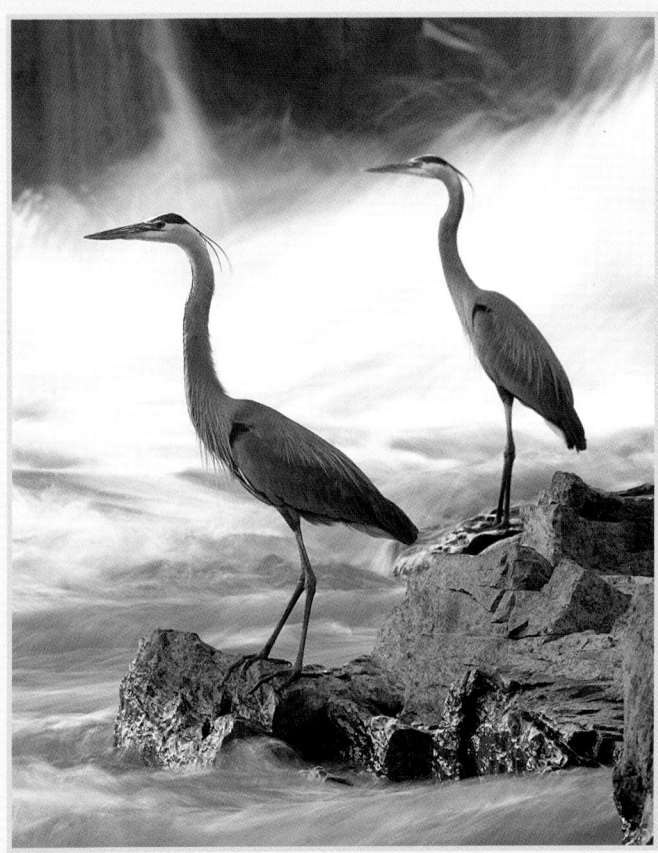

GREAT FALLS OF THE POTOMAC, located on the Maryland/Virginia border, is truly one of the wonders of the world. Here, great blue herons plunge into the turbulent waters, disappearing for a moment only to dramatically reemerge with a fish. Kayakers also brave the raging rapids, surfing in the waters below the Falls – with the occasional expert daring to run the Falls themselves. The view to the left is of the "Spout", one of the many rapids at Great Falls.

Next pages: Expert kayakers Mike Mathwin, Eric Brooks, and Adam Cramer run the Falls.

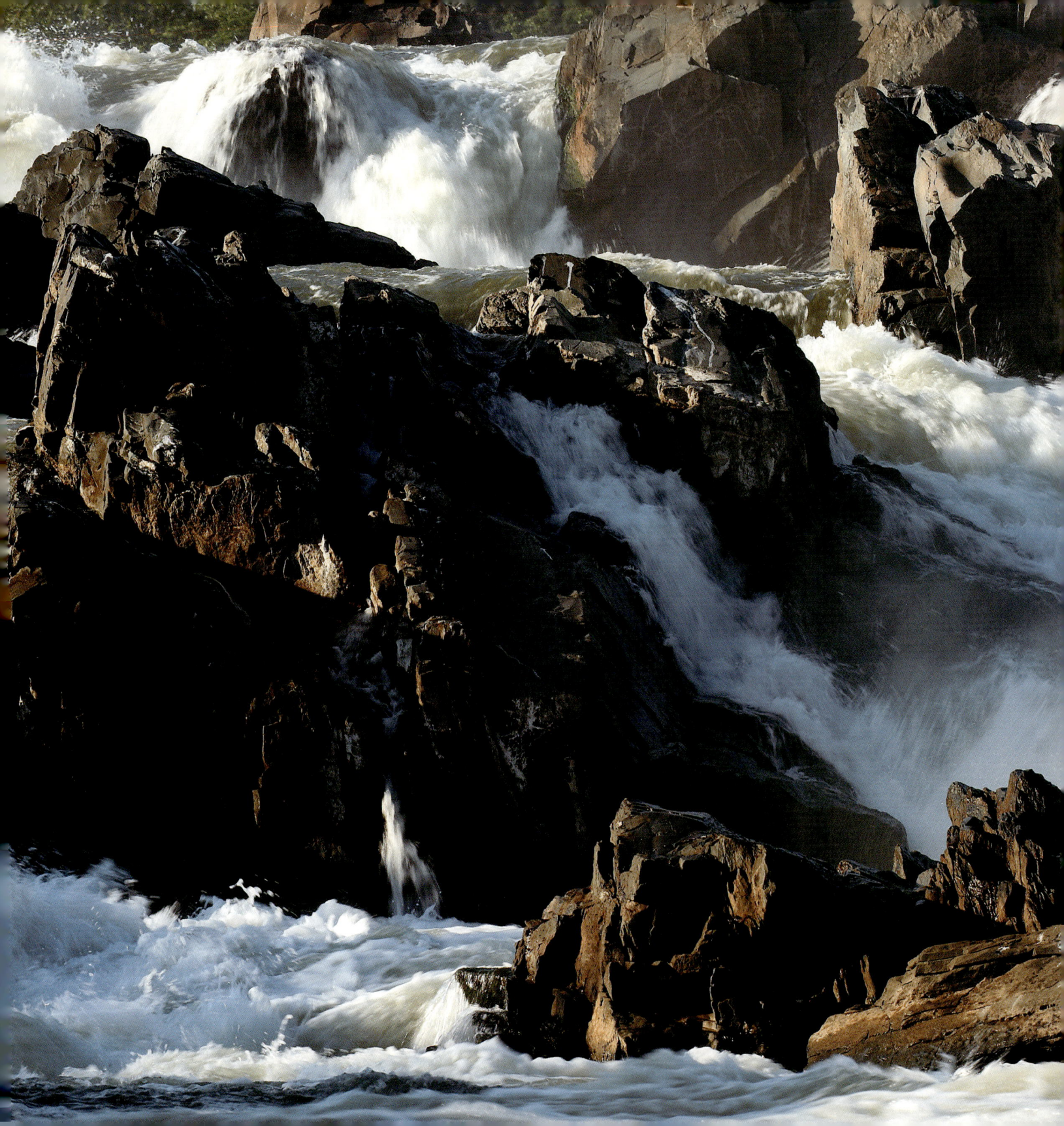

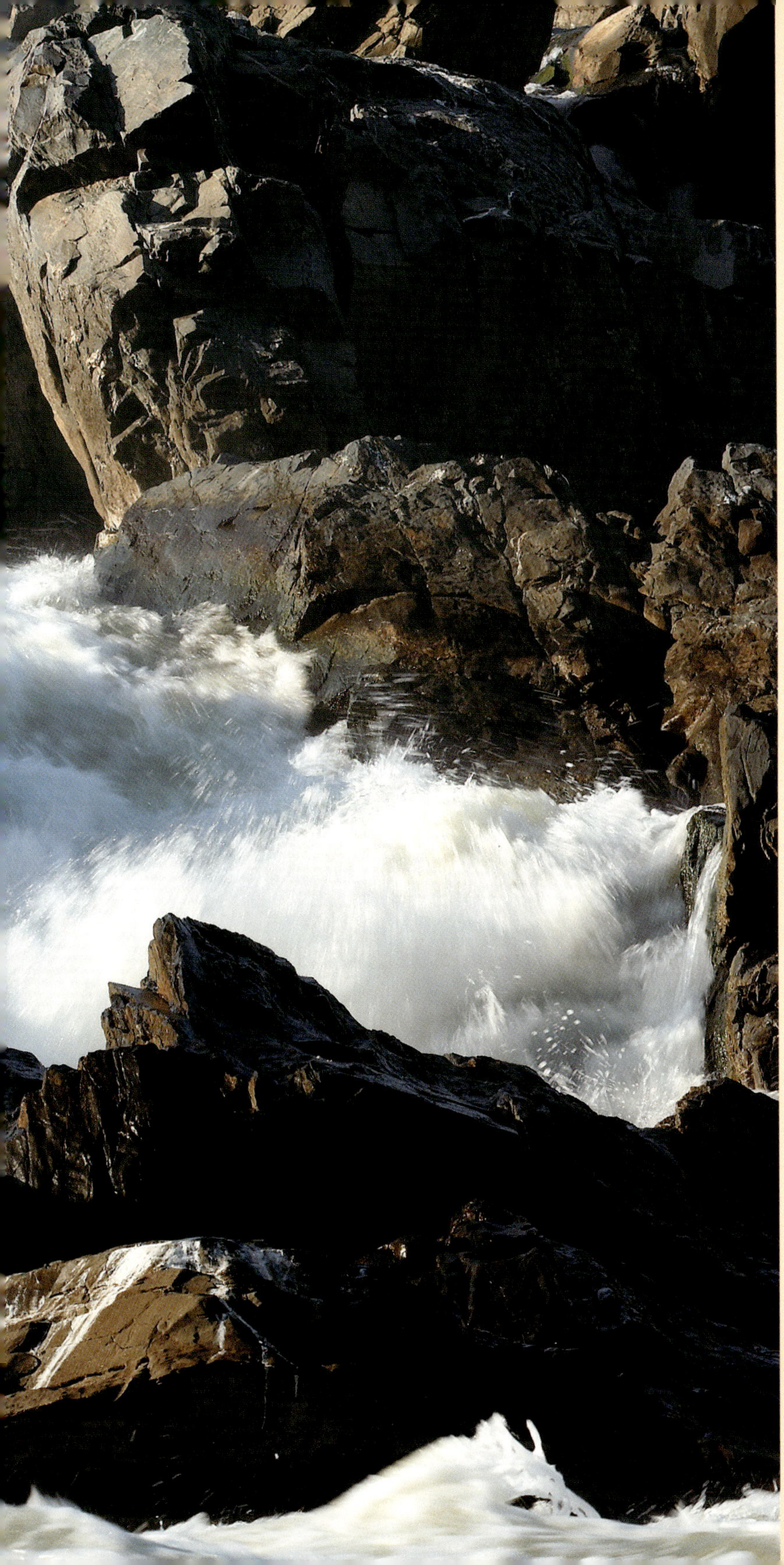

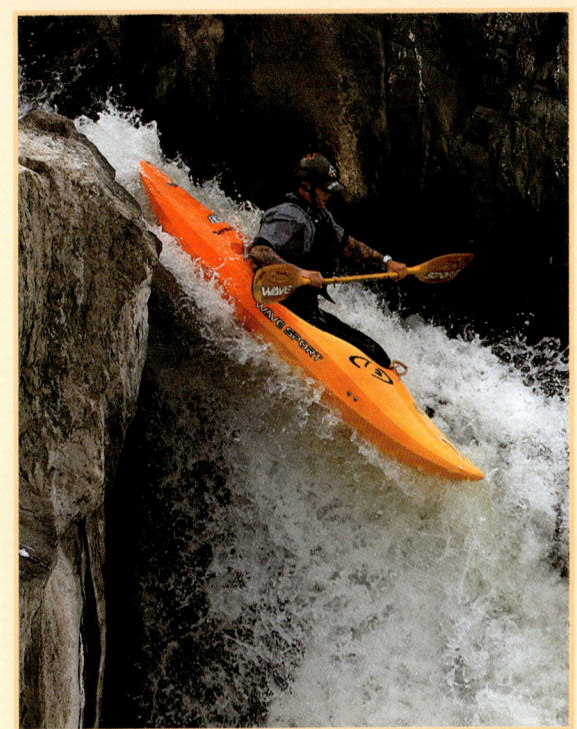

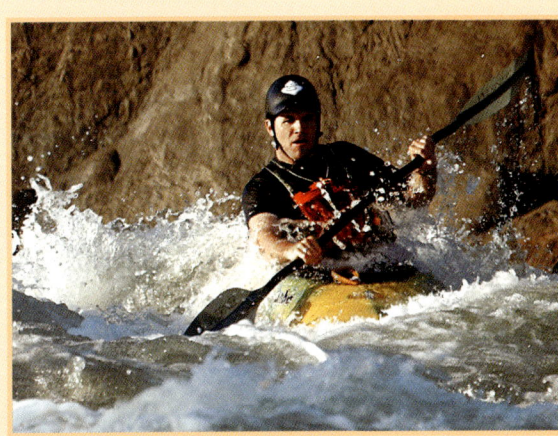

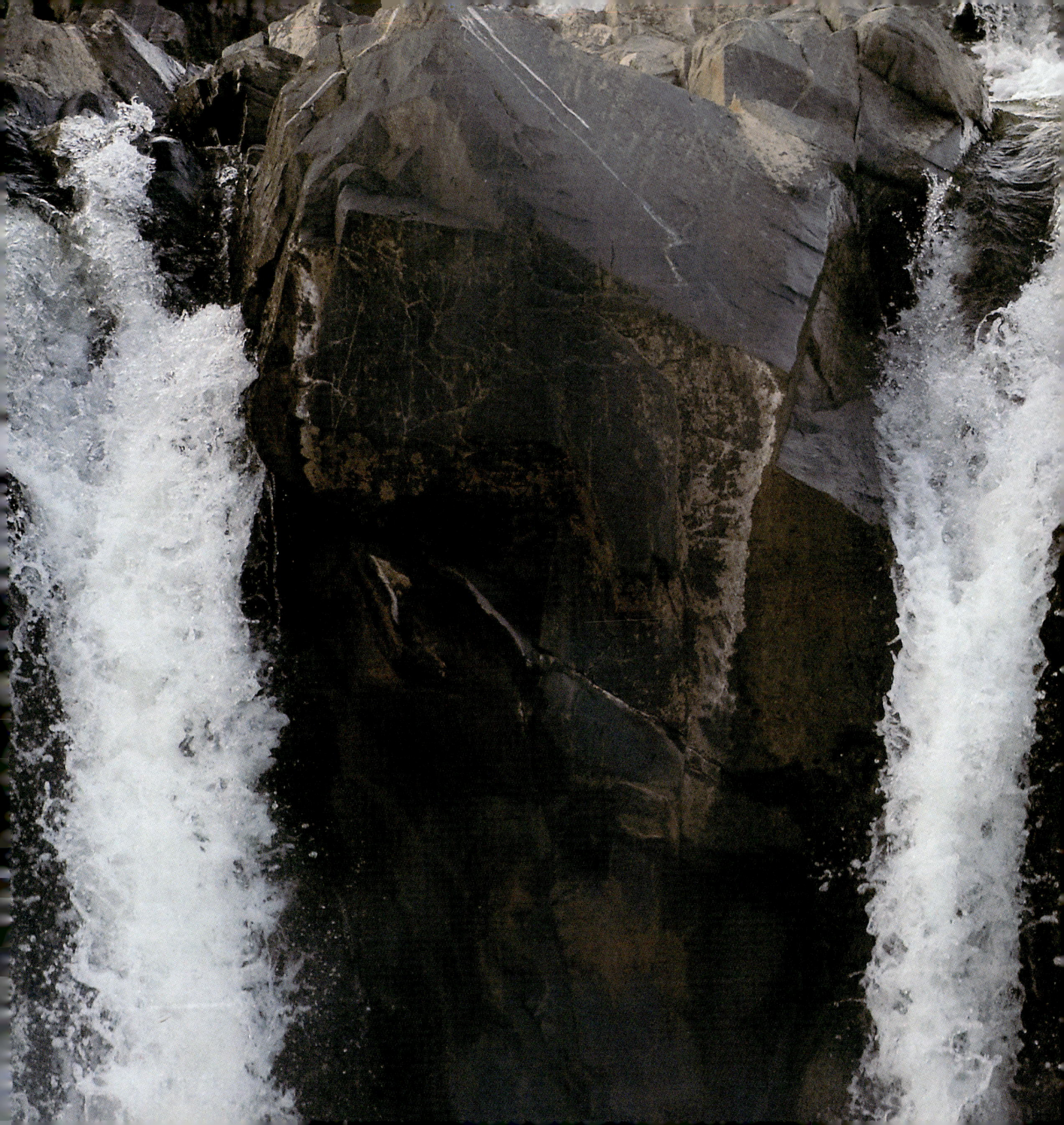

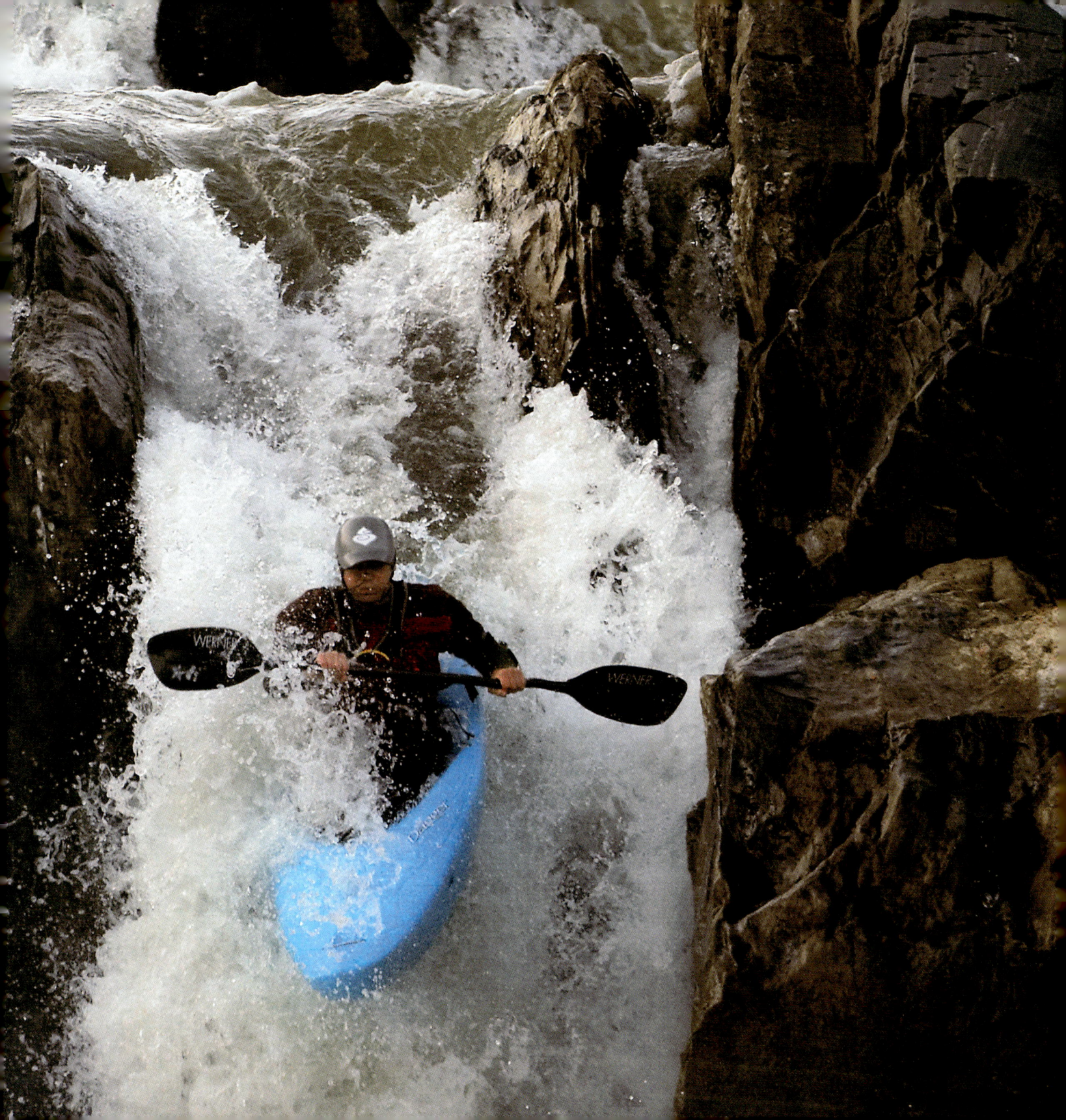

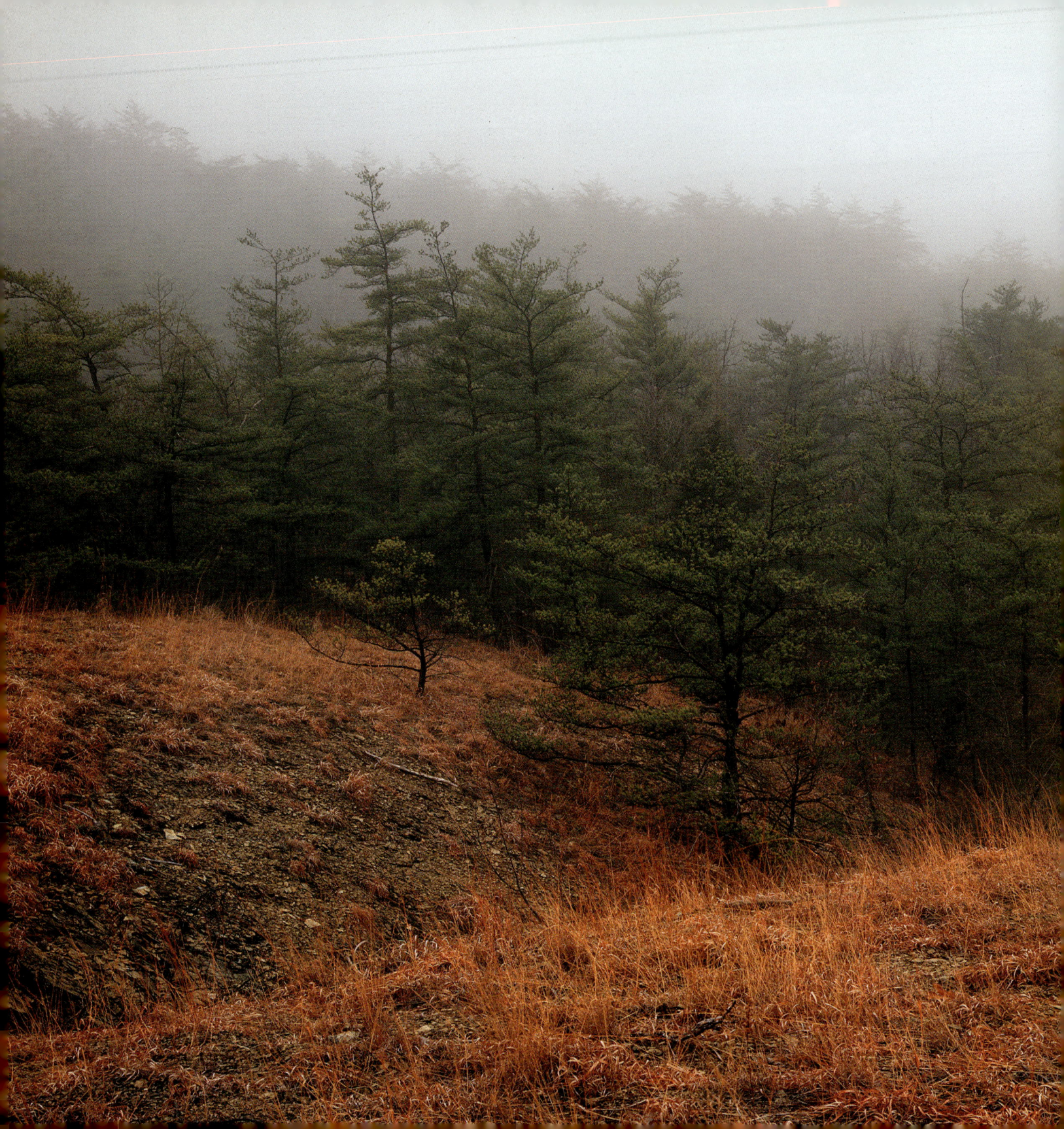

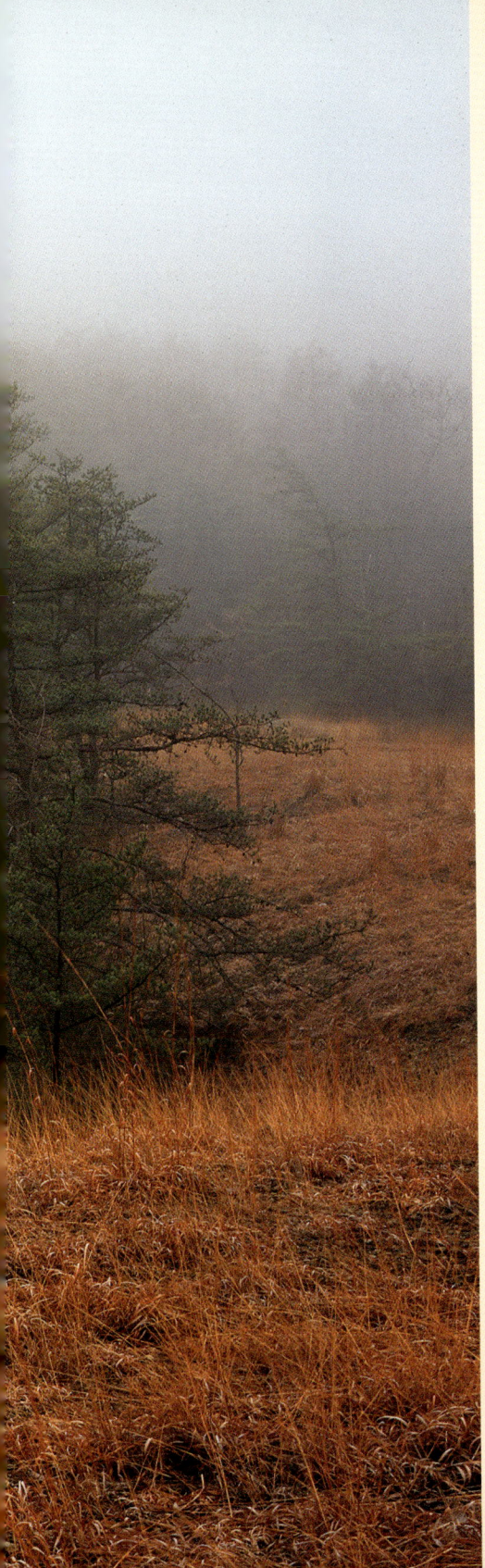

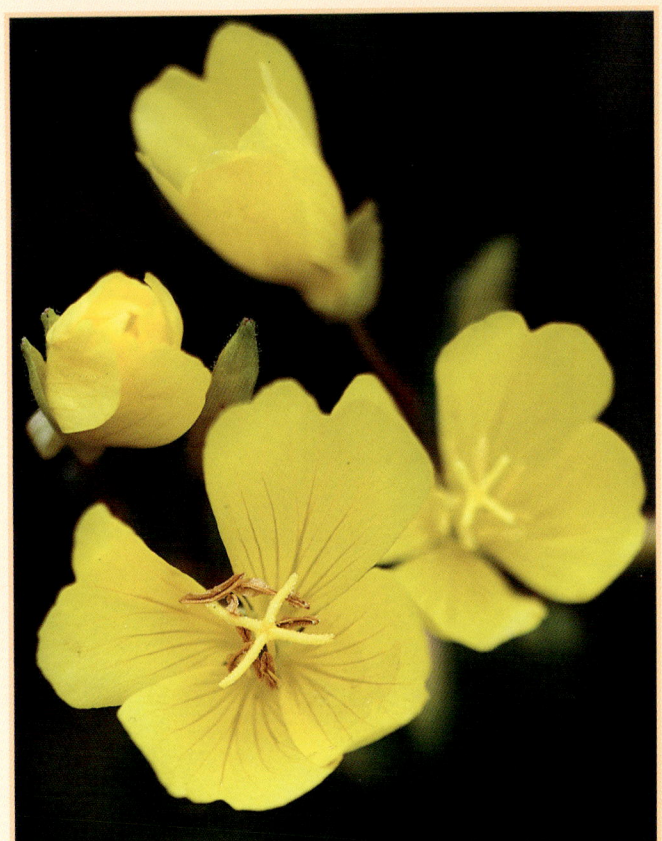

S OLDIERS DELIGHT Natural Environment Area is comprised of 1,900 acres of serpentine barren. The bedrock is underlain with serpentine, a rock high in magnesium and deficient in essential plant nutrients. Accordingly, many plant species that are otherwise prolific in Maryland struggle to survive here, whereas certain grassland species thrive. The area has over 39 rare, threatened, or endangered plant species as well as rare insects, rocks and minerals.

Above: Evening primrose blooms in summer at Soldiers Delight.

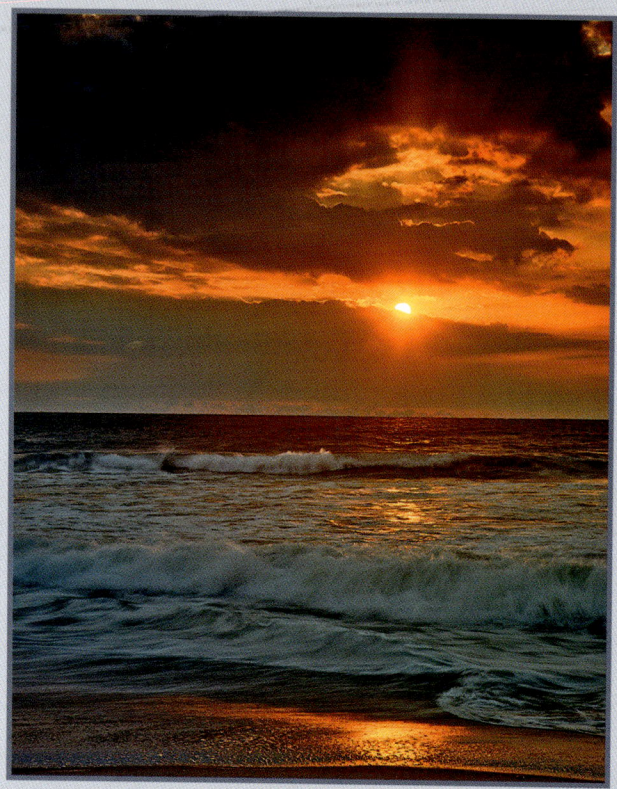

T HE TIMELESS – and seemingly endless – shores of Assateague Island stretch into the infinite Atlantic horizon. Assateague is a barrier island, serving as a continuous, curving barrier against the often devastating waves and wind of the Atlantic Ocean. Storm and sea constantly shape and re-shape Assateague Island, which like every other barrier island is constantly moving and changing.

Despite its desert-like appearance, Assateague is home to abundant wildlife, the most famous of which are wild ponies. The origin of the ponies on Assateague is unclear. The most romantic tales tell of wrecked Spanish galleons and Conquistador horses struggling through the surf to shore, but more likely the ponies are descended from herds maintained by early colonial mainland farmers who used the island's waters as a natural fence.

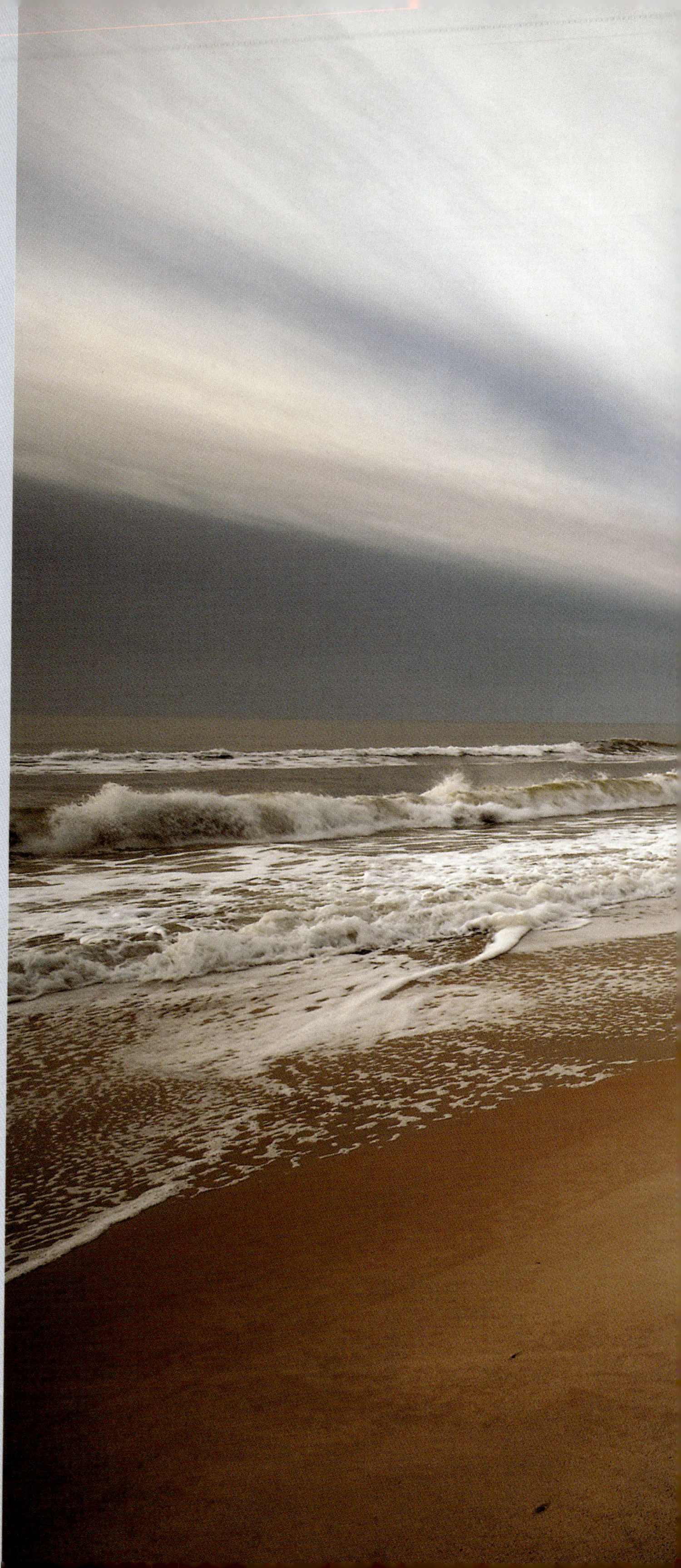

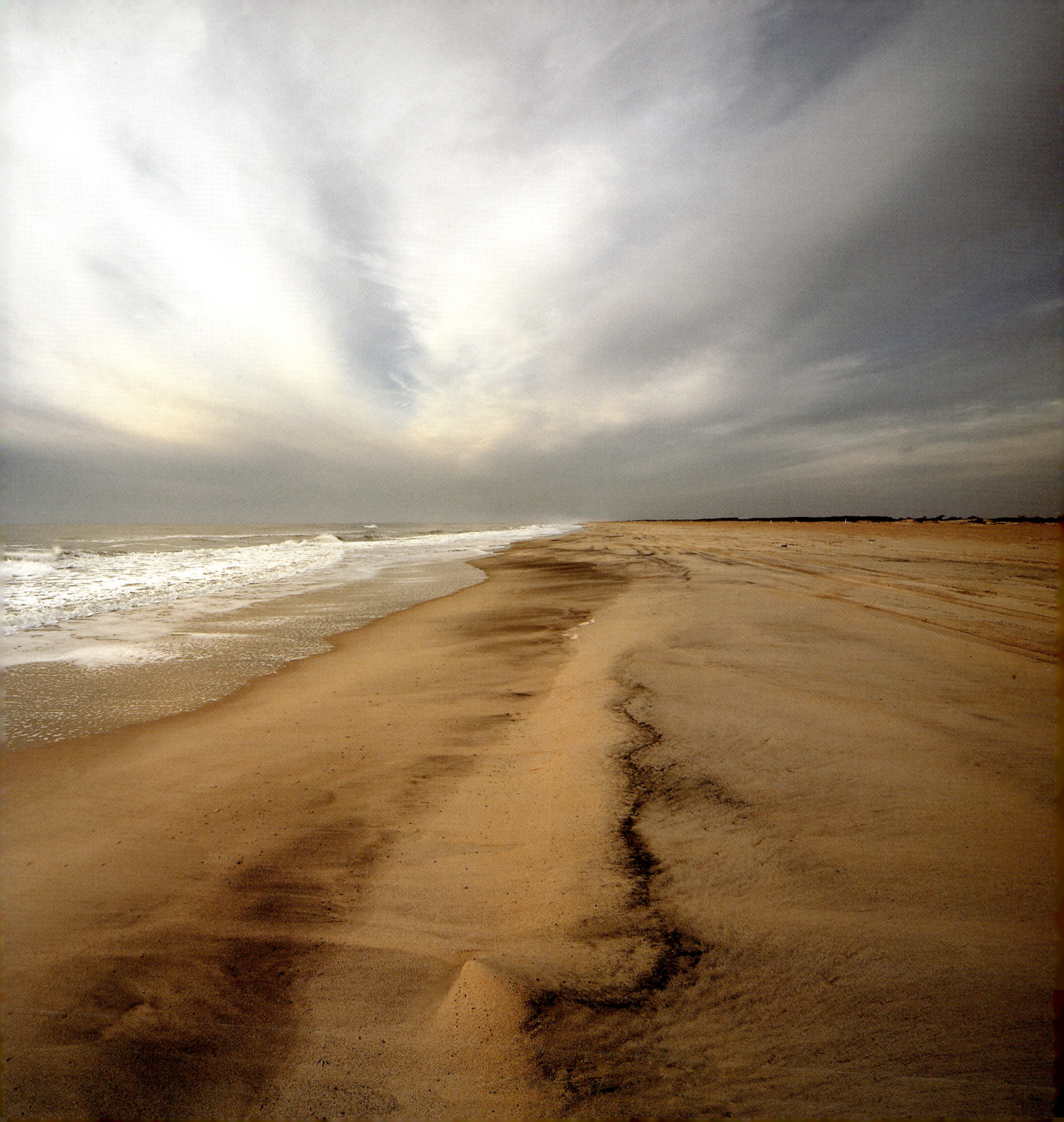

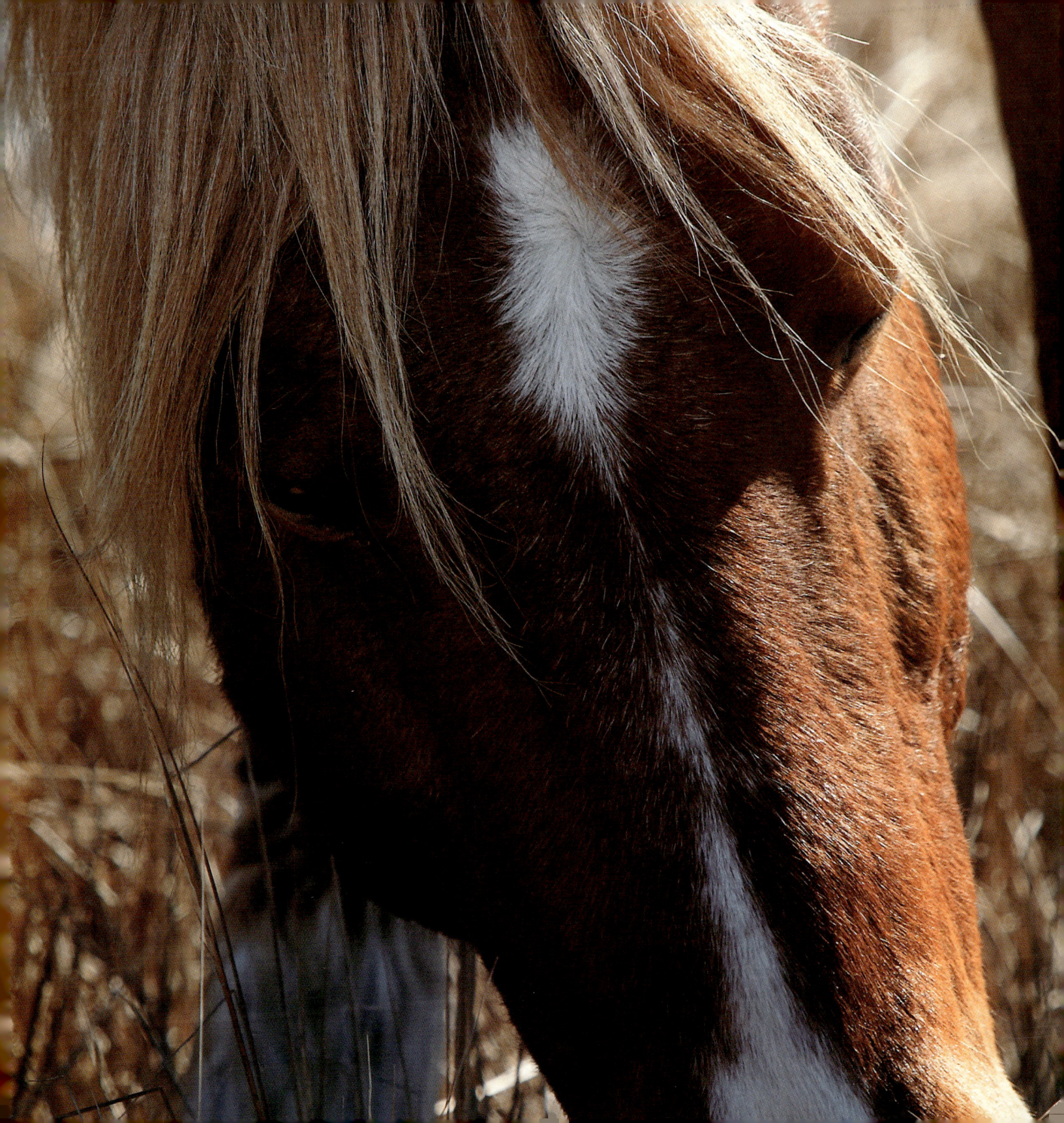

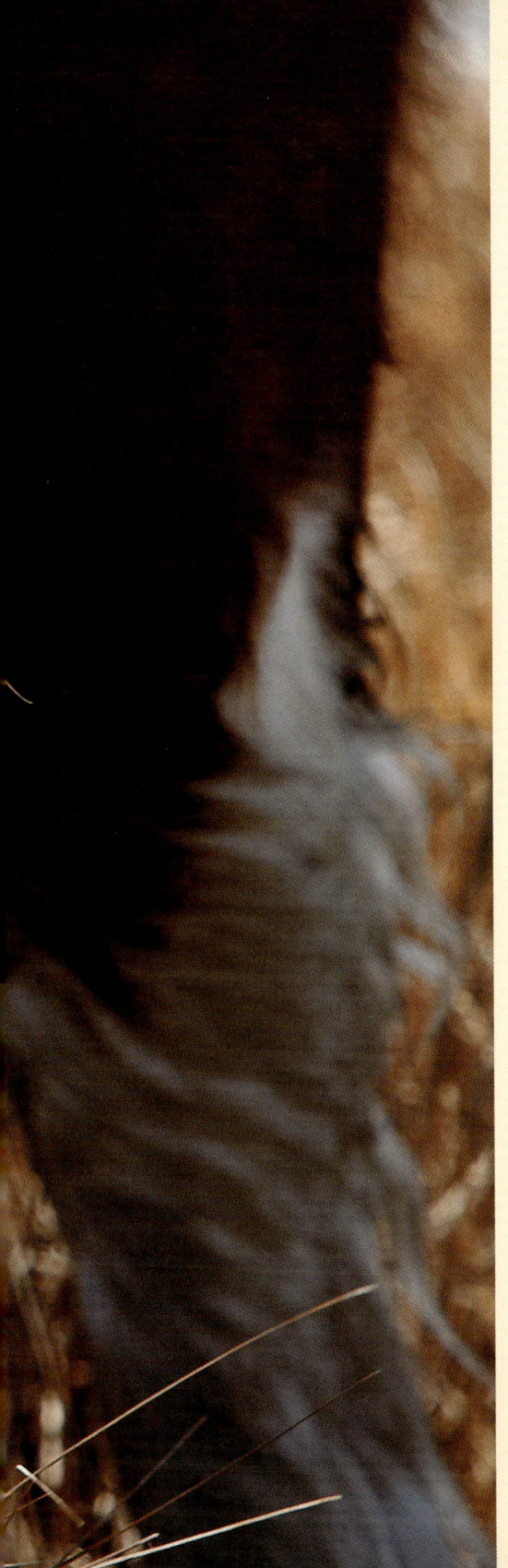
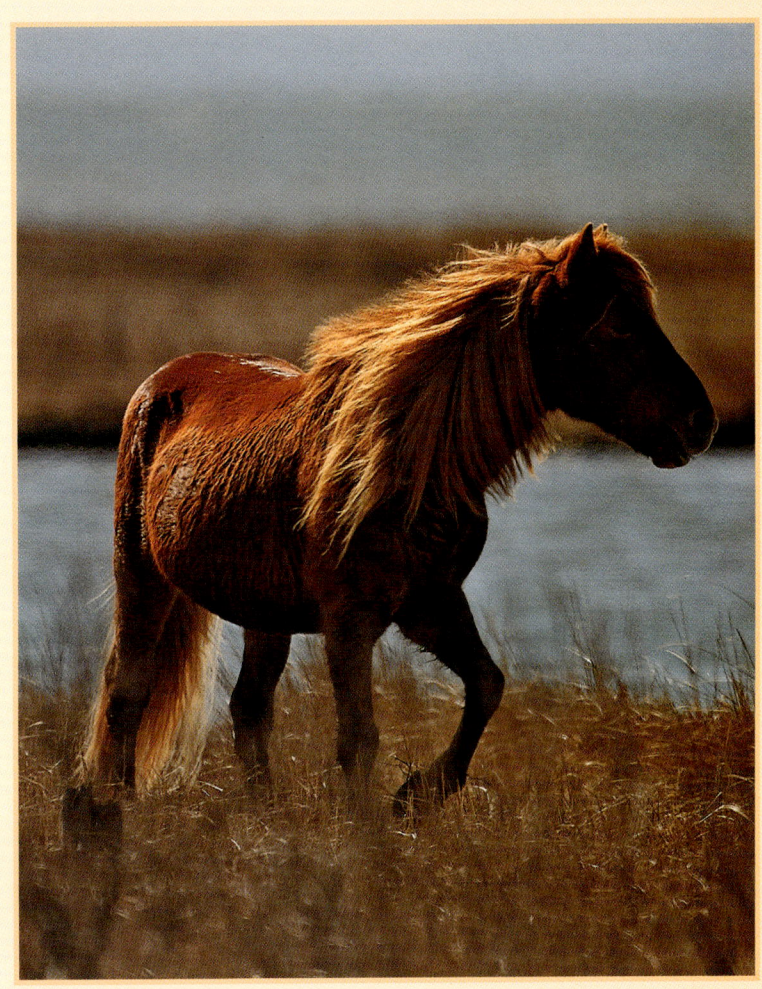

The famous wild ponies of Assateague Island.

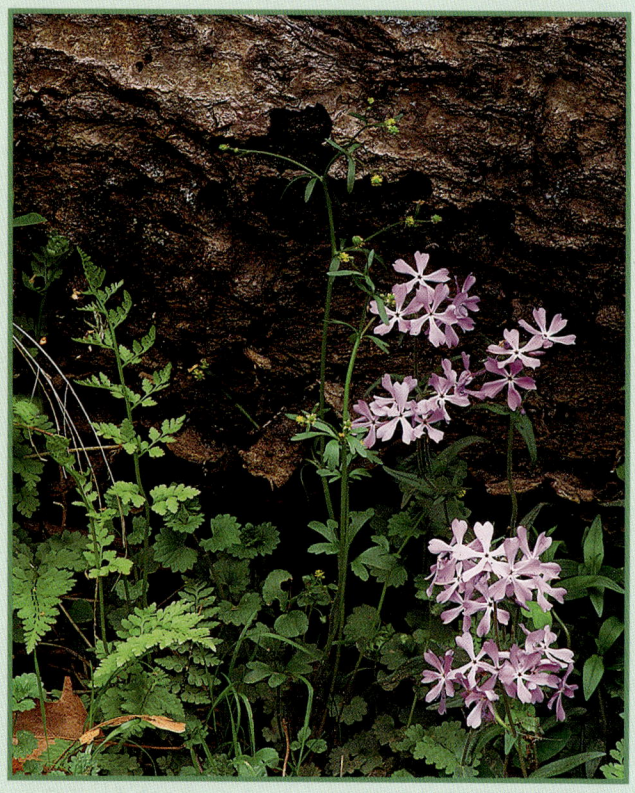

SWALLOW FALLS STATE PARK contains some of Maryland's most breathtaking scenery and unique geological features. At the base of Muddy Creek Falls, several natural arches have formed in a stone column right before the creek plunges into the Youghiogheny River.

Above: Wild blue phlox blooms in the summer.

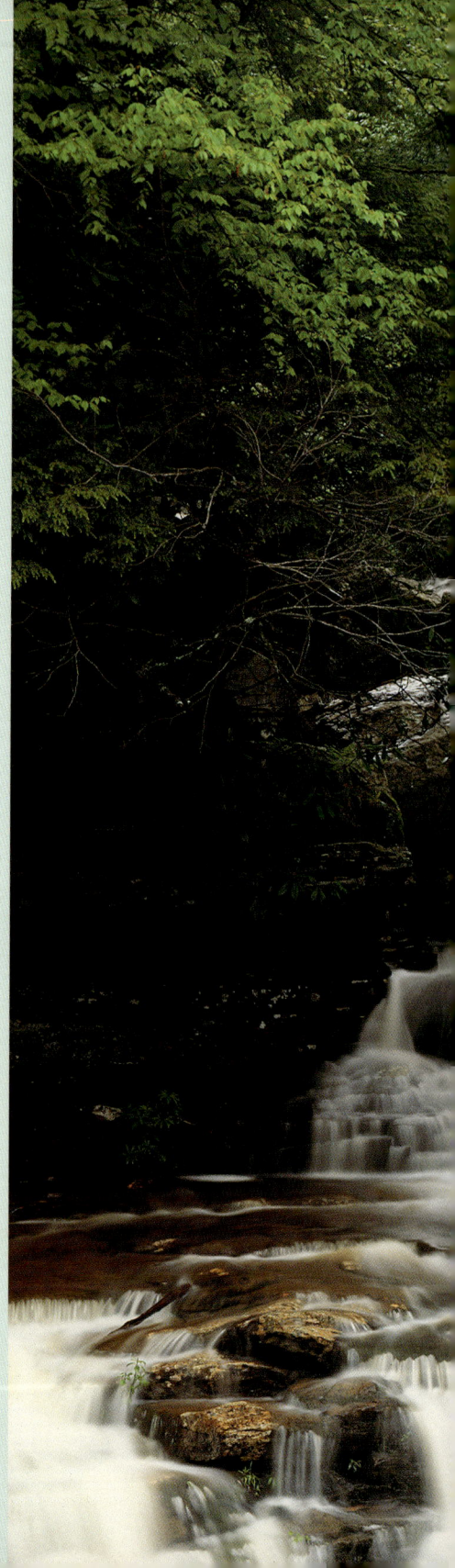

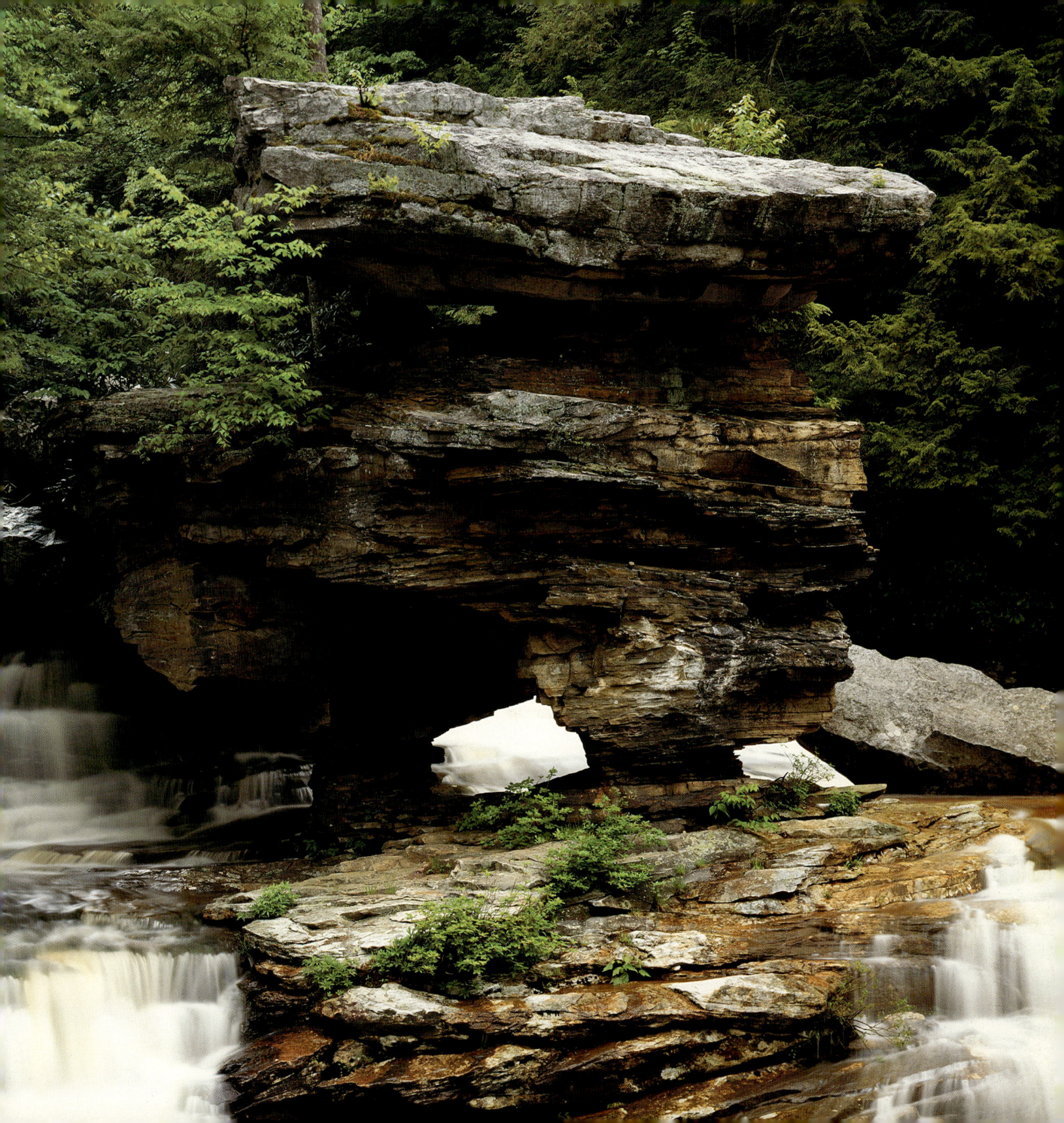

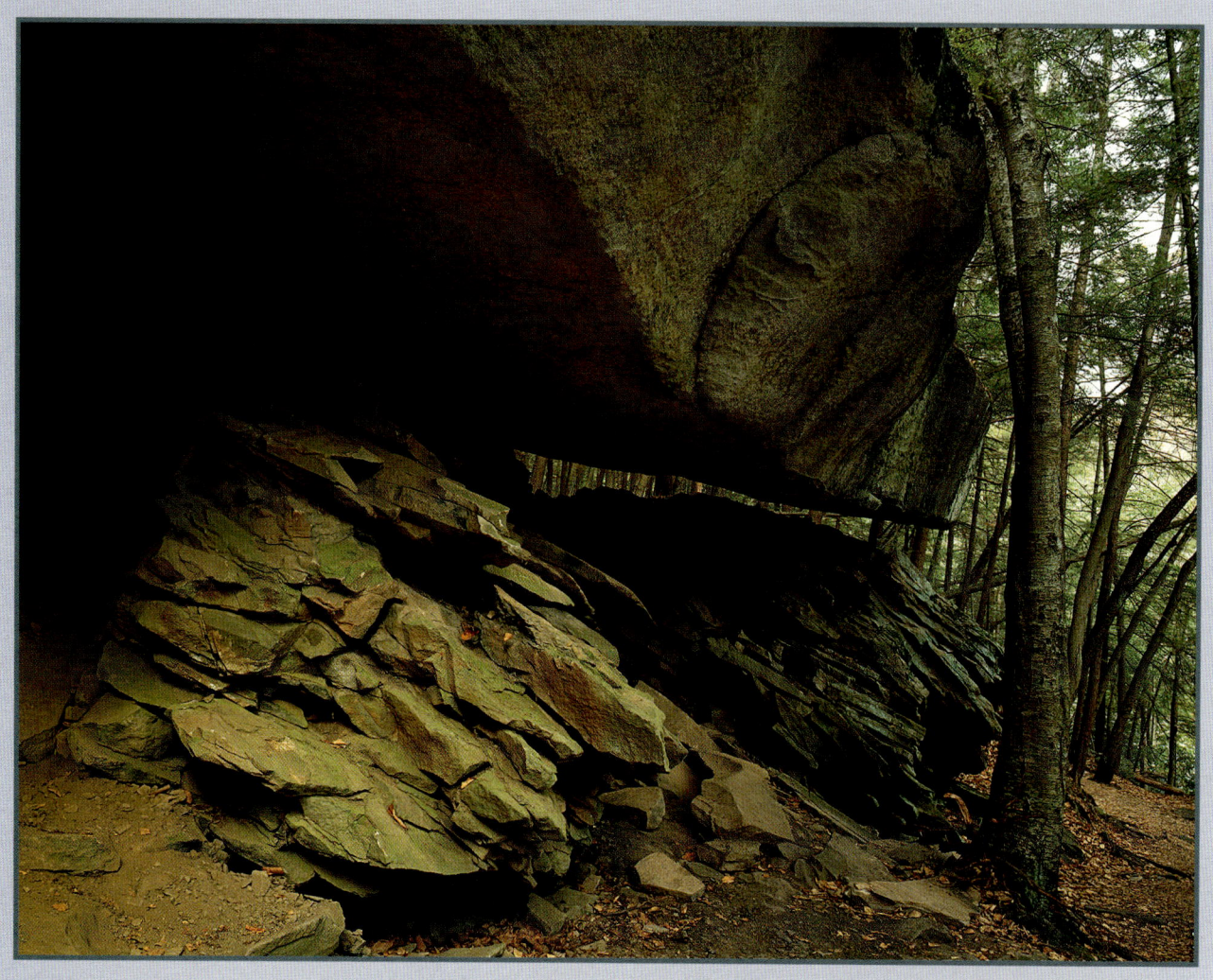

Above: A cave created by an overhanging rock contains some
unusual rock formations in Swallow Falls State Park.

Right: Beneath Muddy Creek Falls, Maryland's
highest single-drop waterfall.

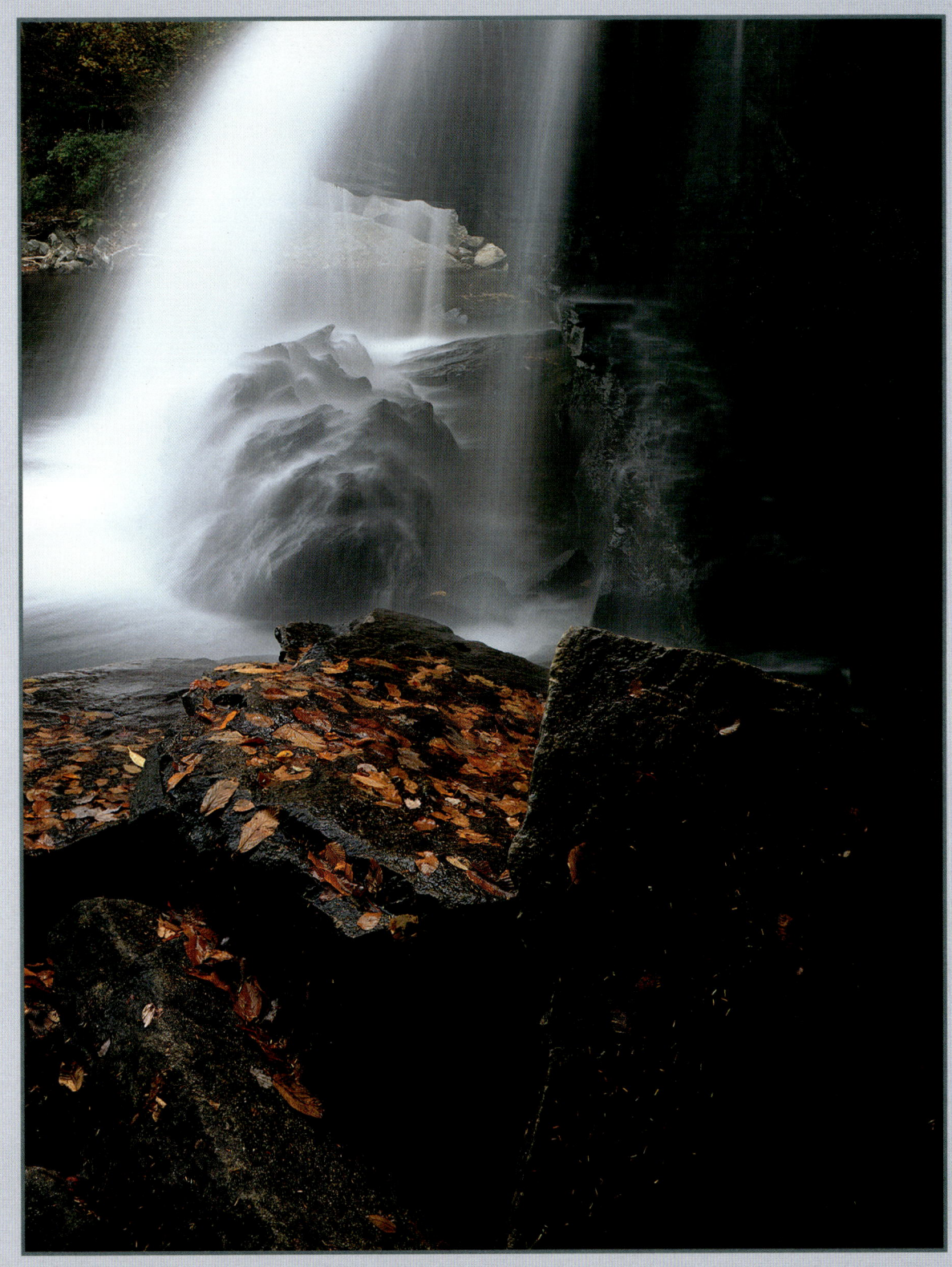

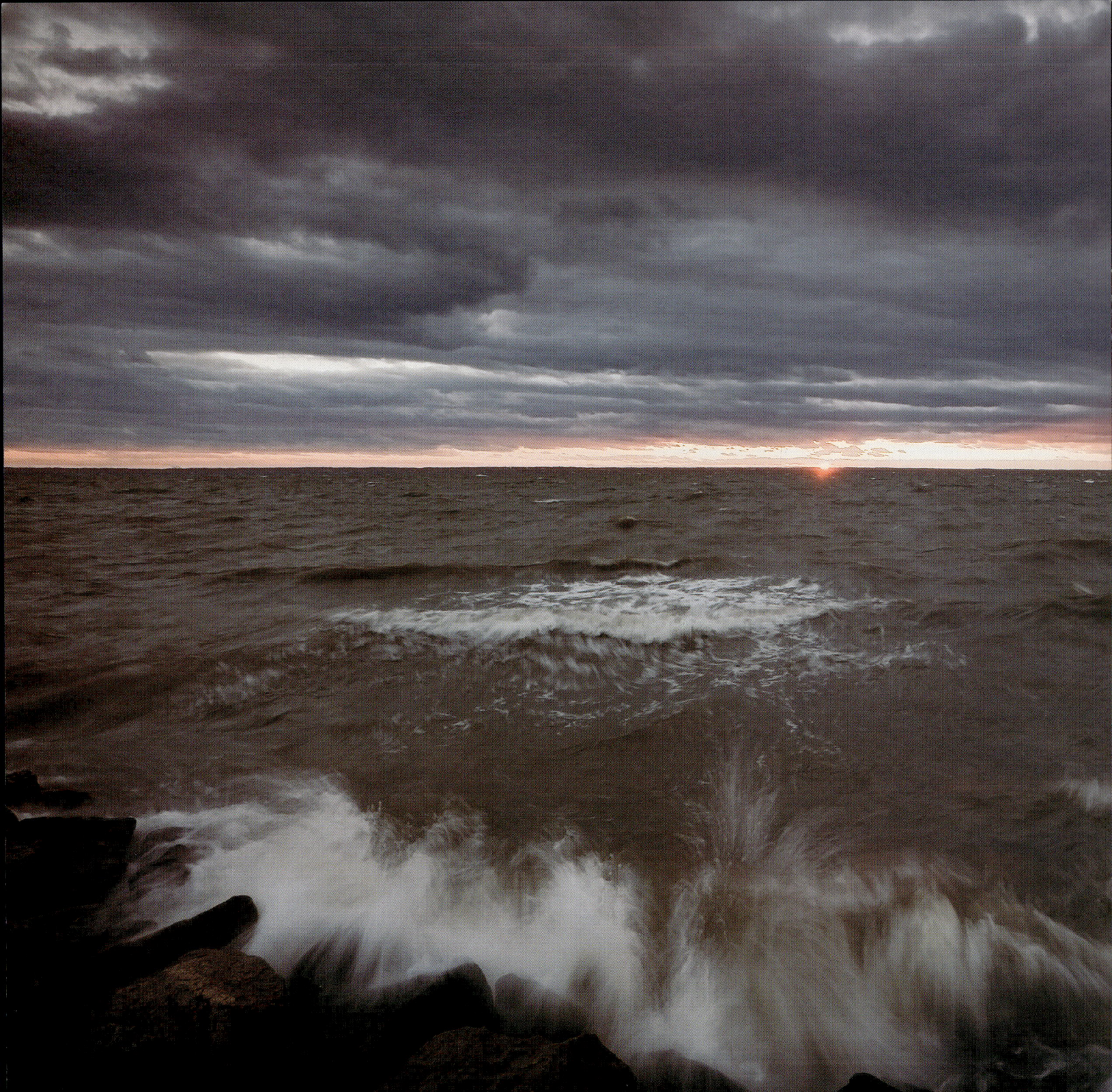

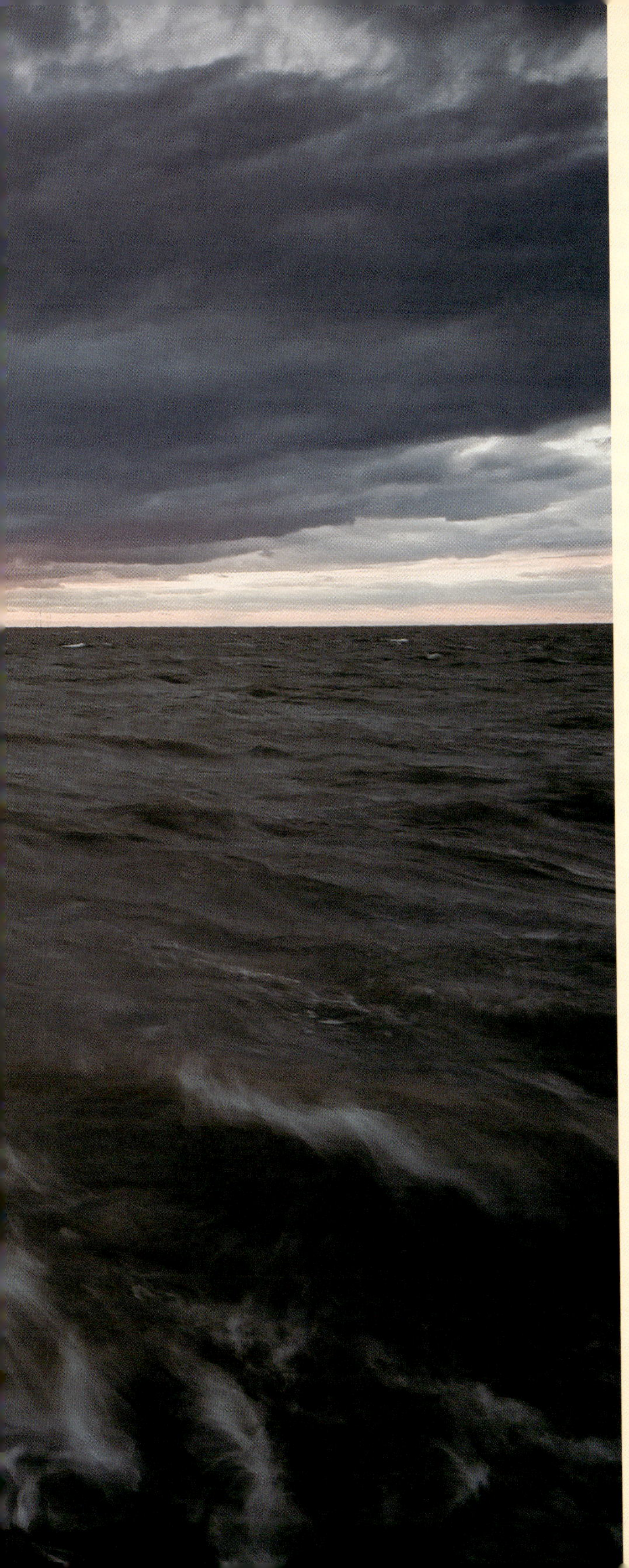

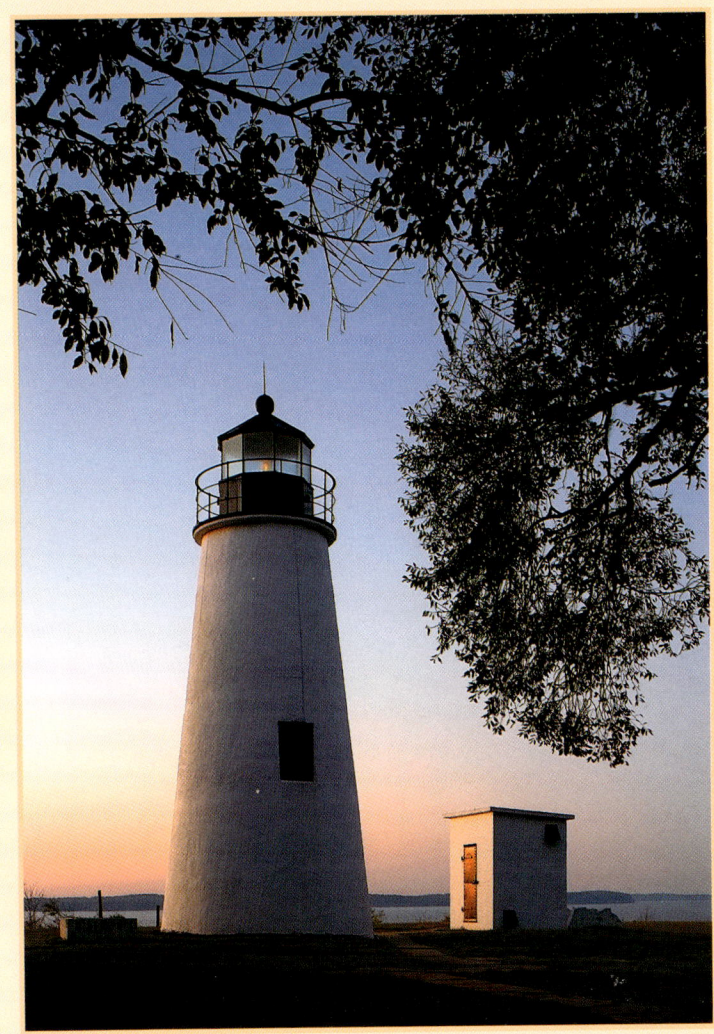

Left: The remnants of a hurricane pass over the Chesapeake Bay, as seen from Tilghman Island on the Eastern Shore.

Above: Turkey Point Lighthouse, located on bluffs high above the Bay, Elk Neck State Park.

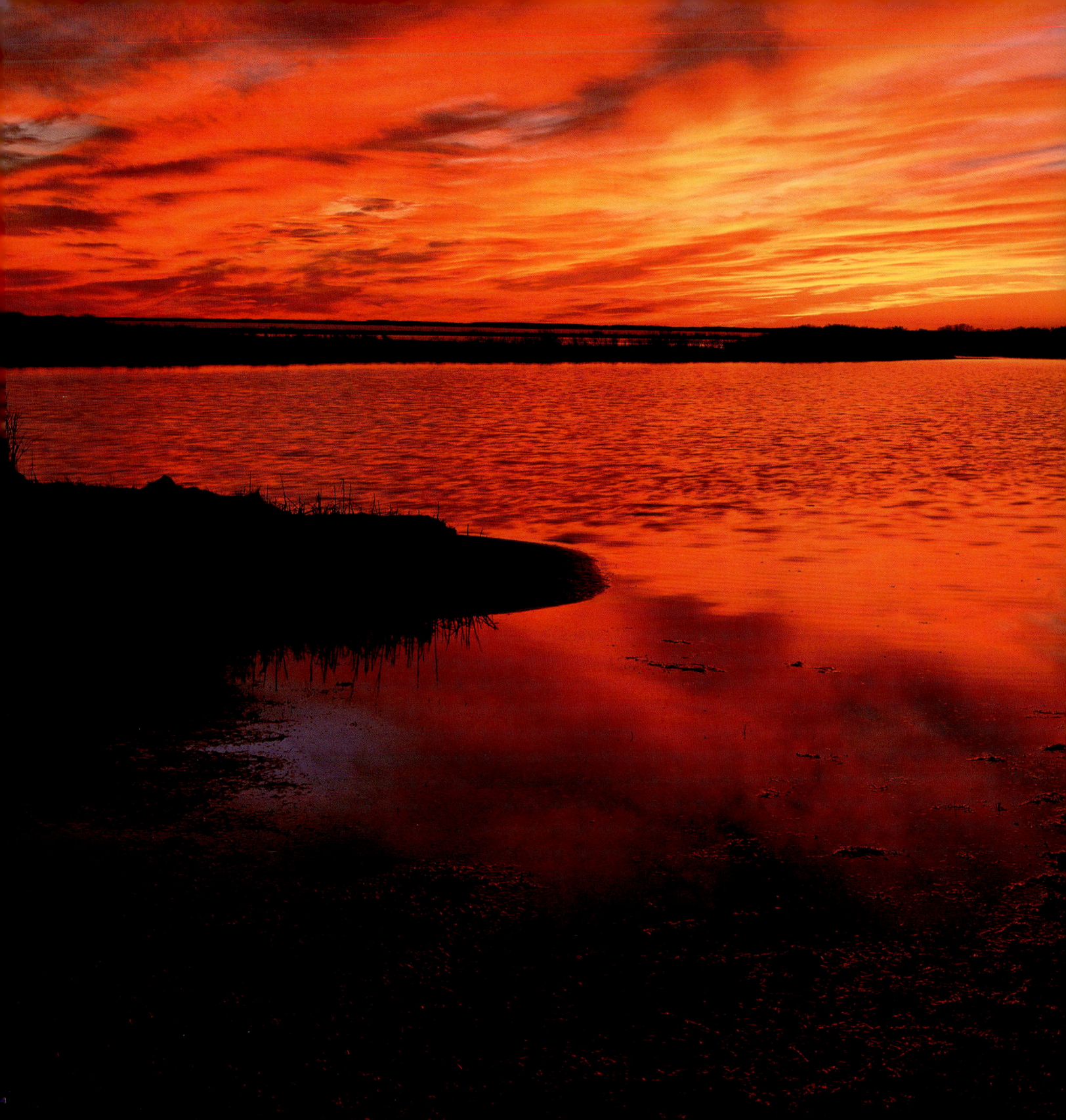

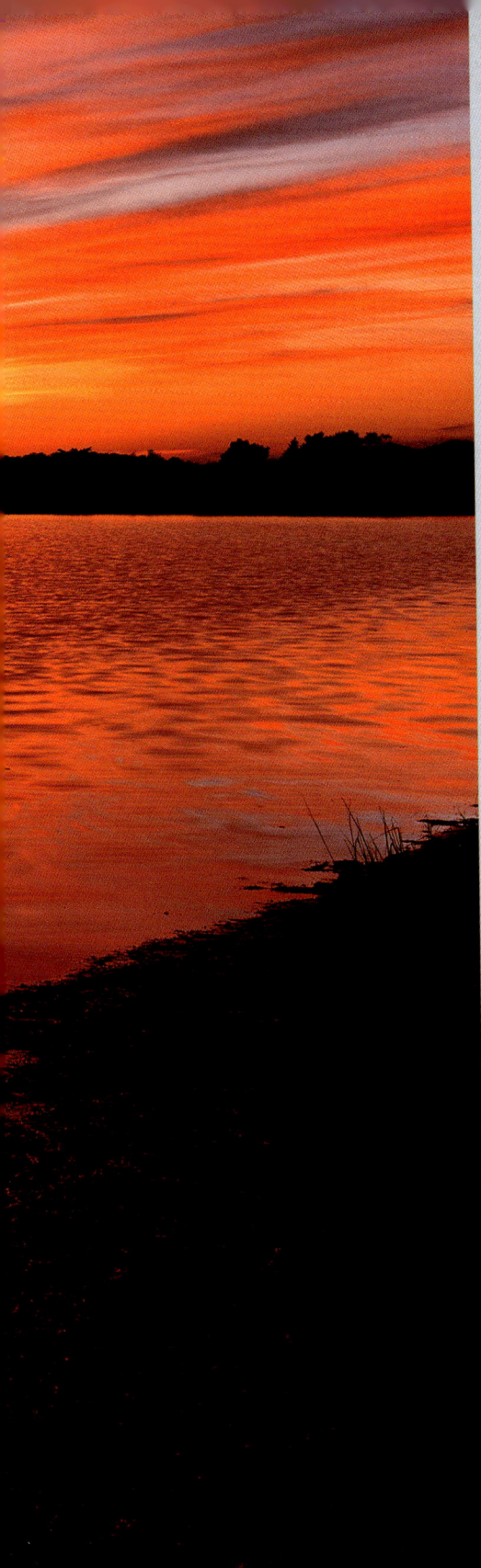

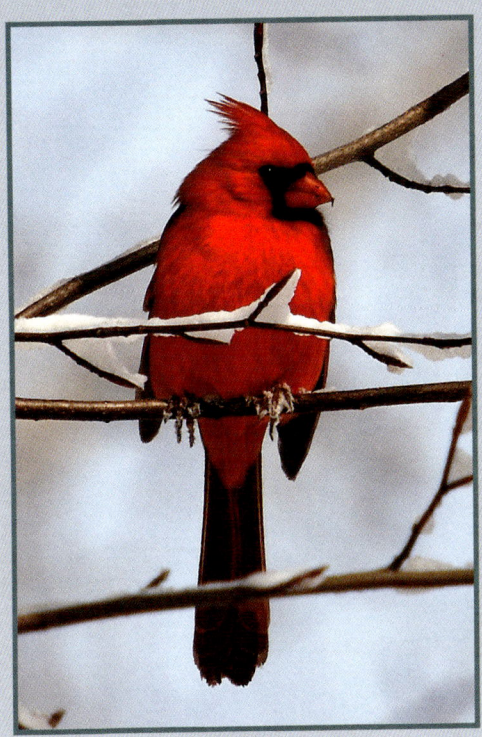

Left: Sunset over tidal marshes on Assateague Island.

Above: A male cardinal clings to a snowy branch.

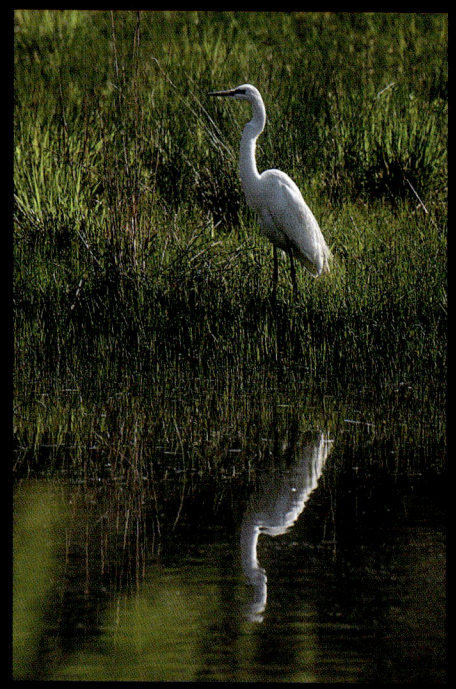

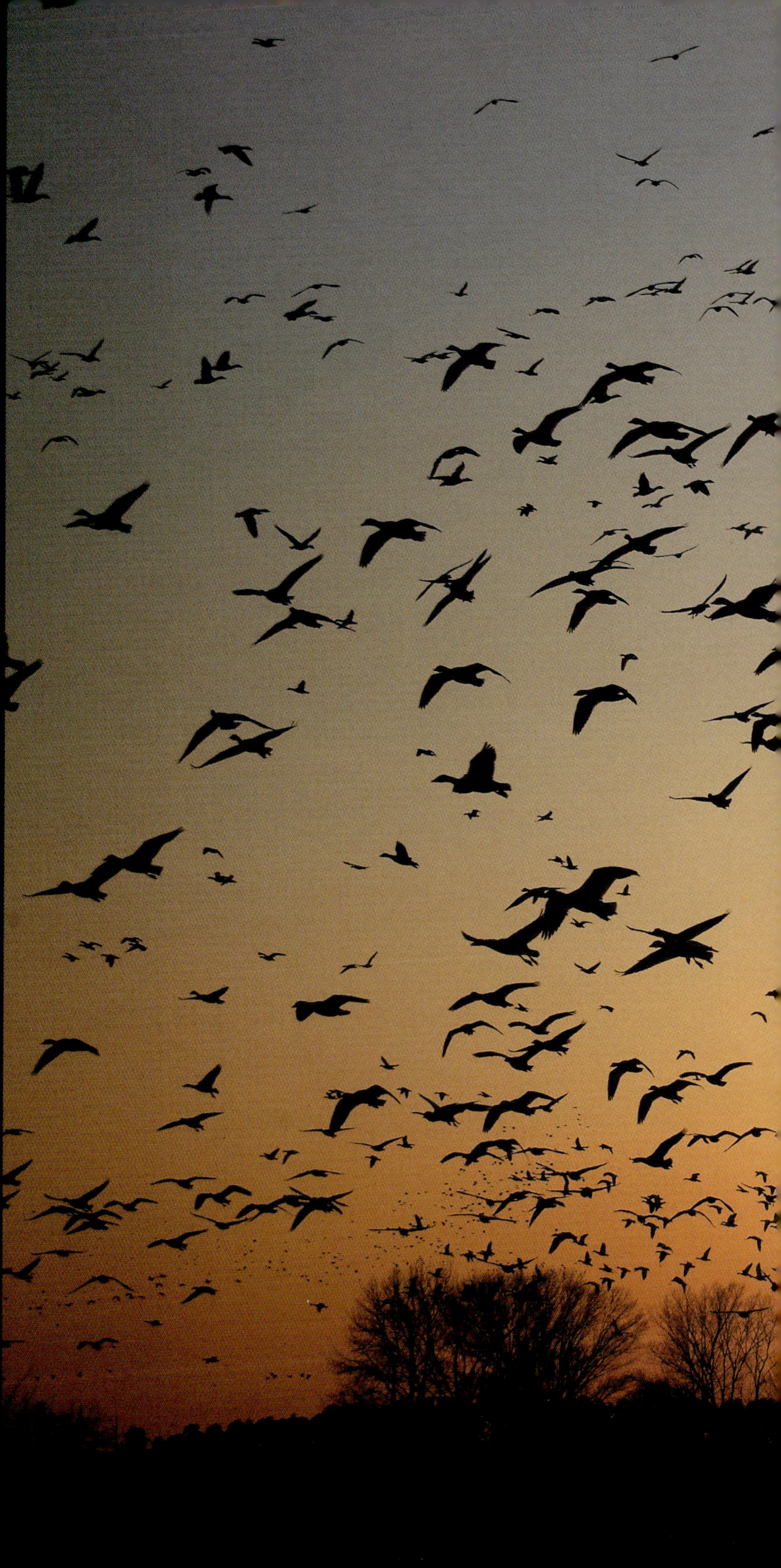

B IRDS COME BY THE THOUSANDS to Blackwater National Wildlife Refuge on the Eastern Shore of Maryland, south of the town of Cambridge in Dorchester County. Blackwater was established in 1933 as a refuge for migratory birds, and today includes over 27,000 acres of rich tidal marsh. During the winter, enormous flocks of geese feed at Blackwater, covering the sky at dusk. During the summer, egrets, herons, and osprey call Blackwater their home. The Refuge also plays host year-round to an abundant bald eagle population.

Above: A great egret searches for prey among Blackwater's rich tidal marshes.

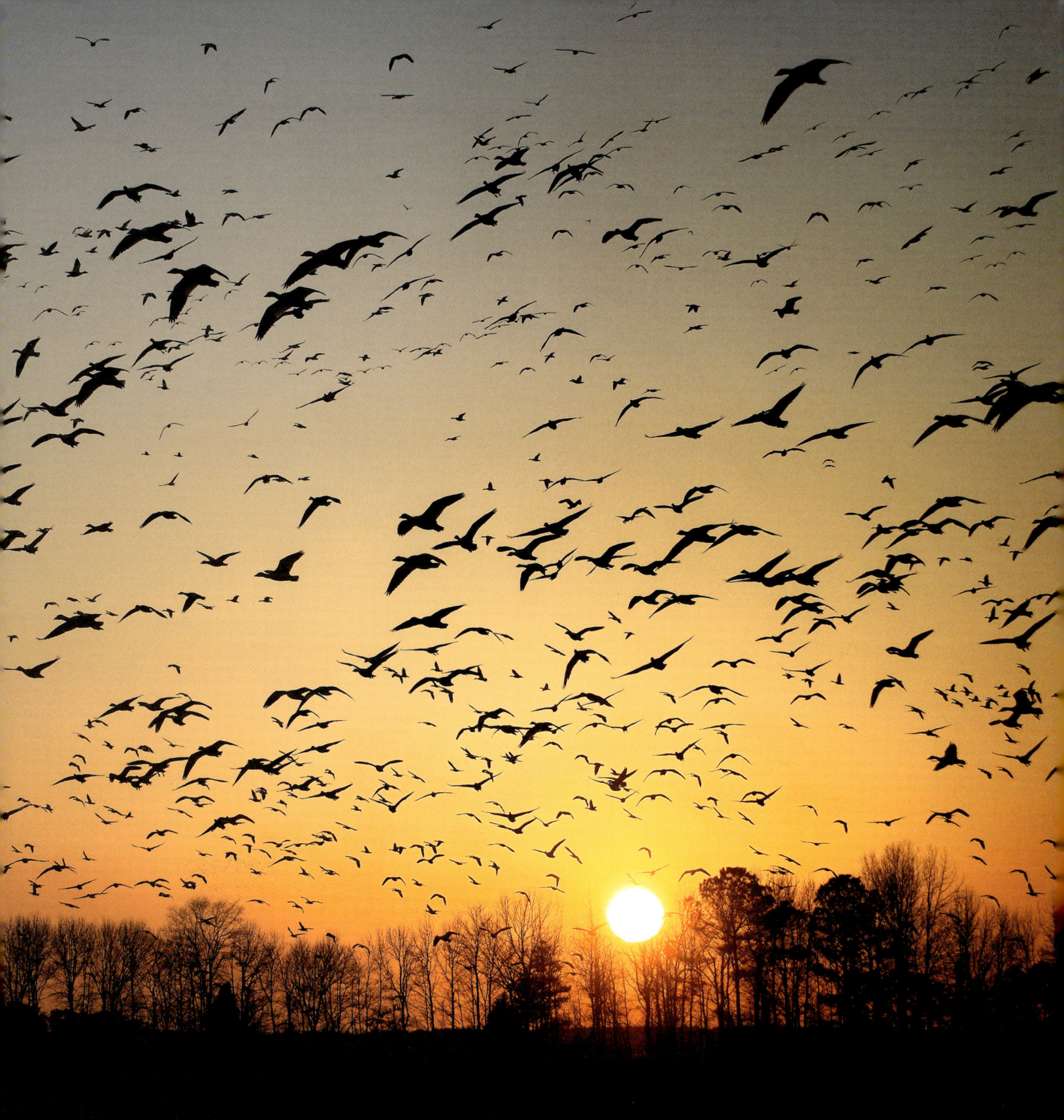

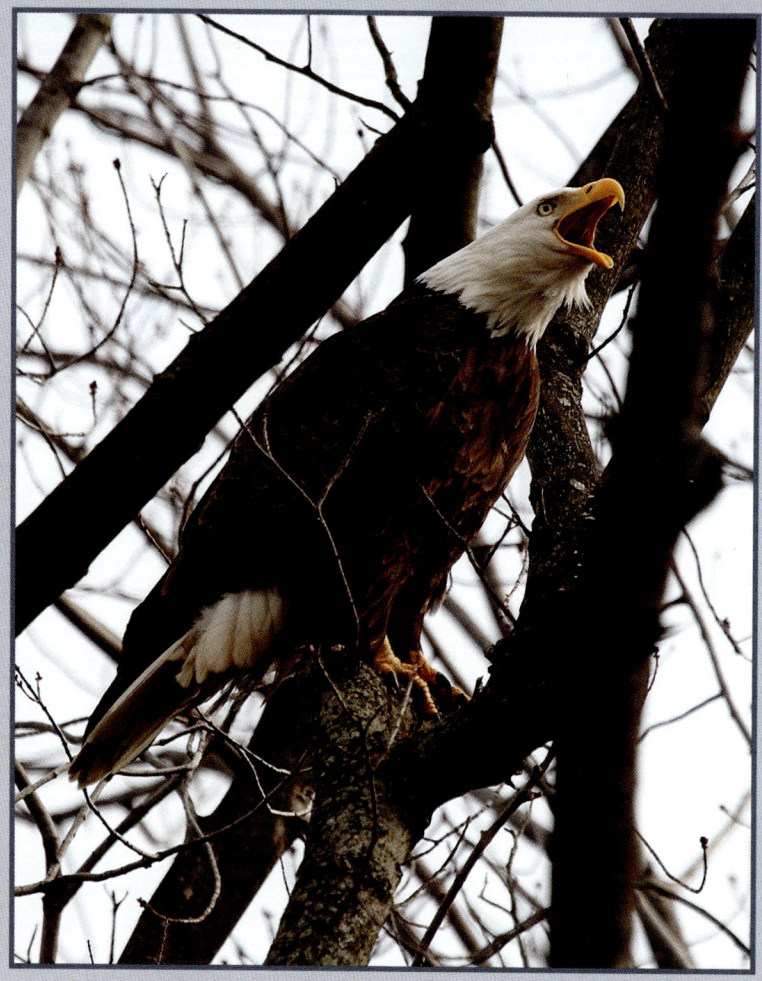

BALD EAGLES, once nearly extinct, are now a common sight along the waterways of Maryland. Our national bird, the bald eagle is the only eagle unique to North America. The bald eagle nearly went extinct because of habitat destruction, illegal shooting, and contamination of its food source (most notably due to the pesticide DDT, which interfered with the eagle's reproduction). Through the banning of DDT, and through other conservation efforts including the protection of habitat such as Blackwater National Wildlife Refuge, eagles now thrive.

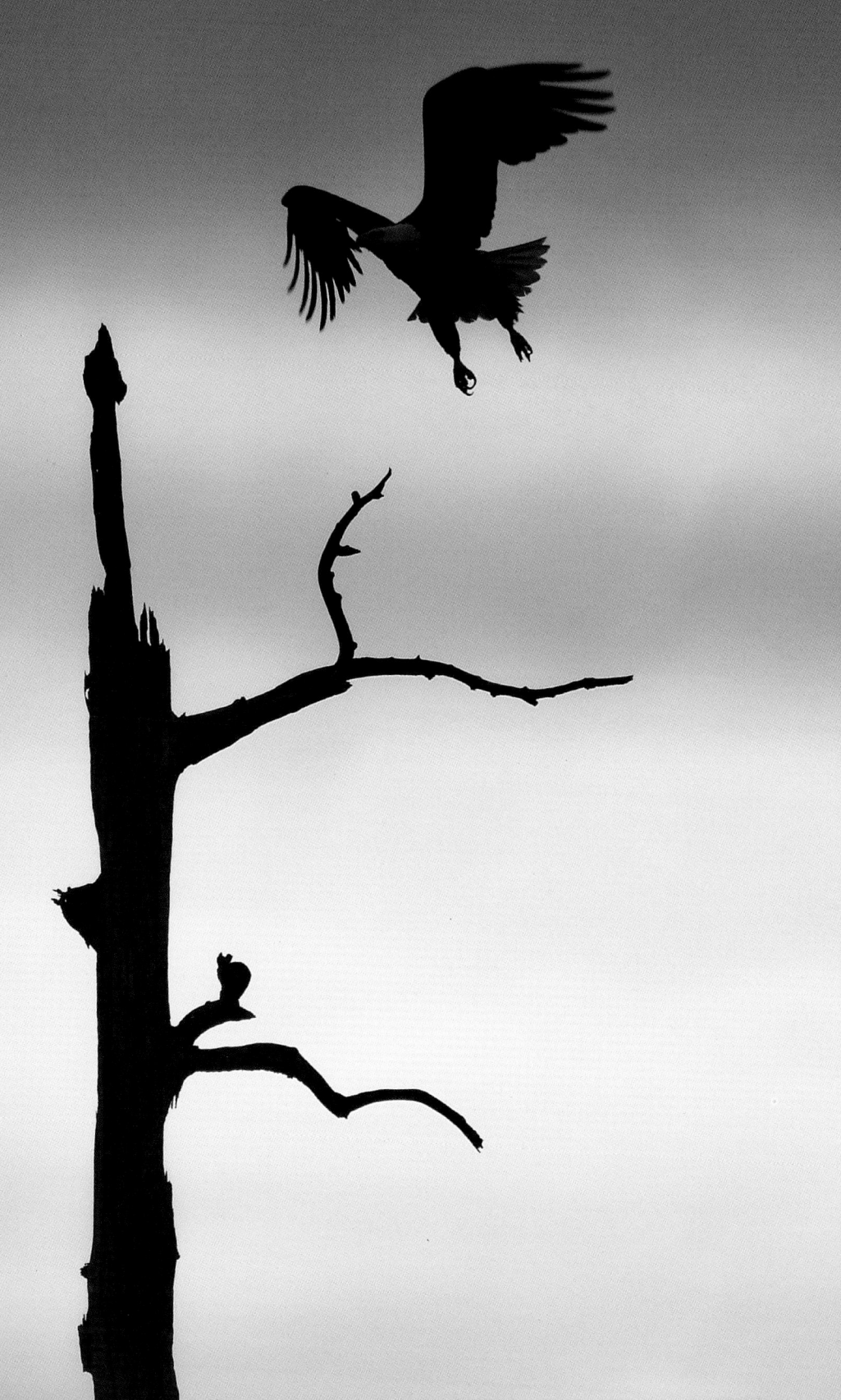

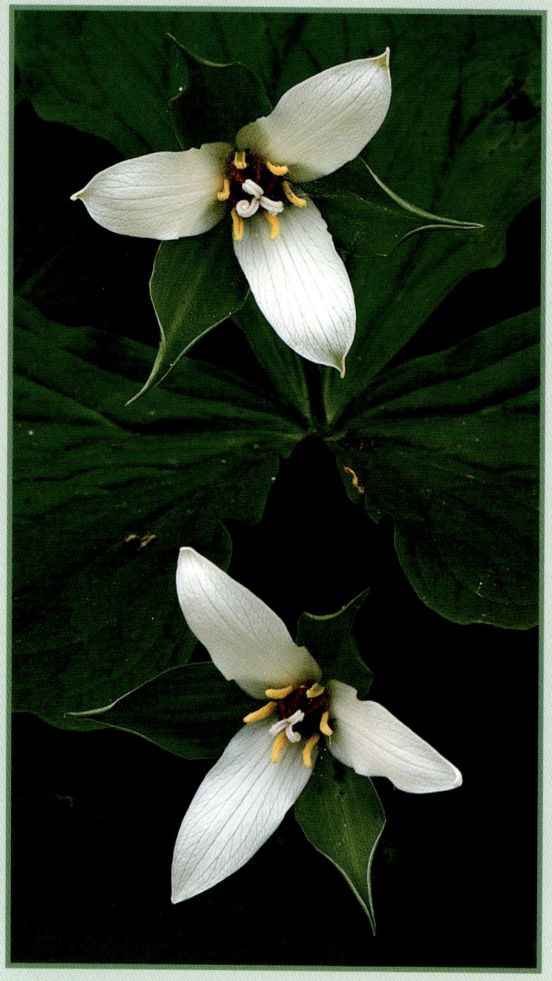

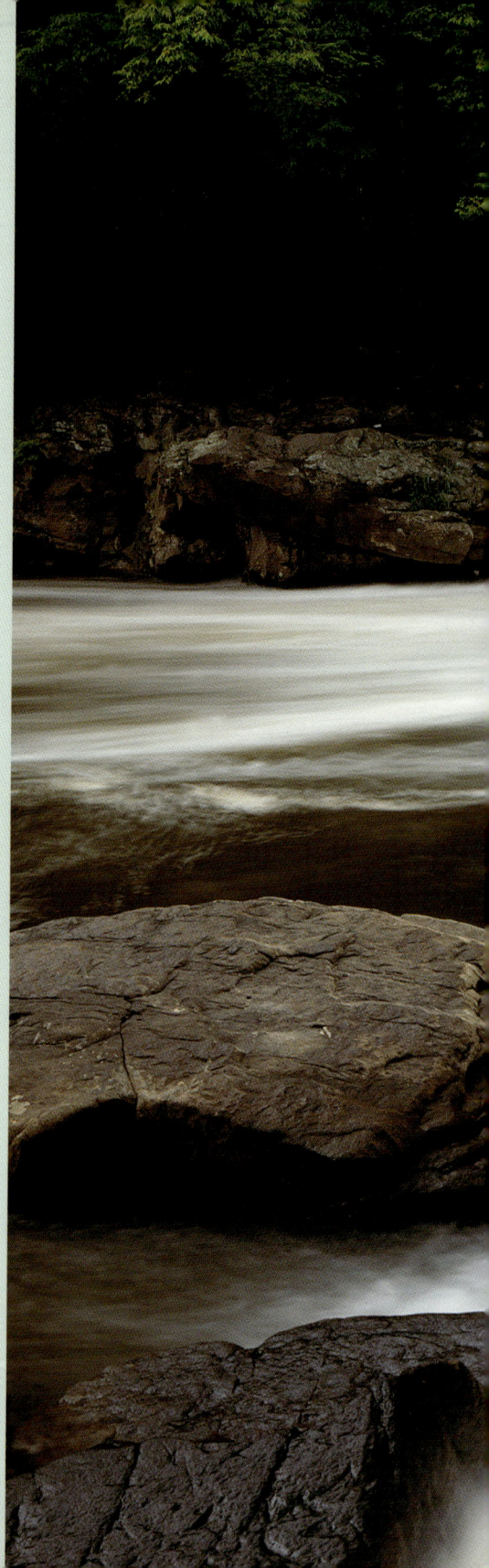

Above: Trillium blooms in spring along the banks of the Susquehanna River.

Right: Upper Swallow Falls, located in Swallow Falls State Park.

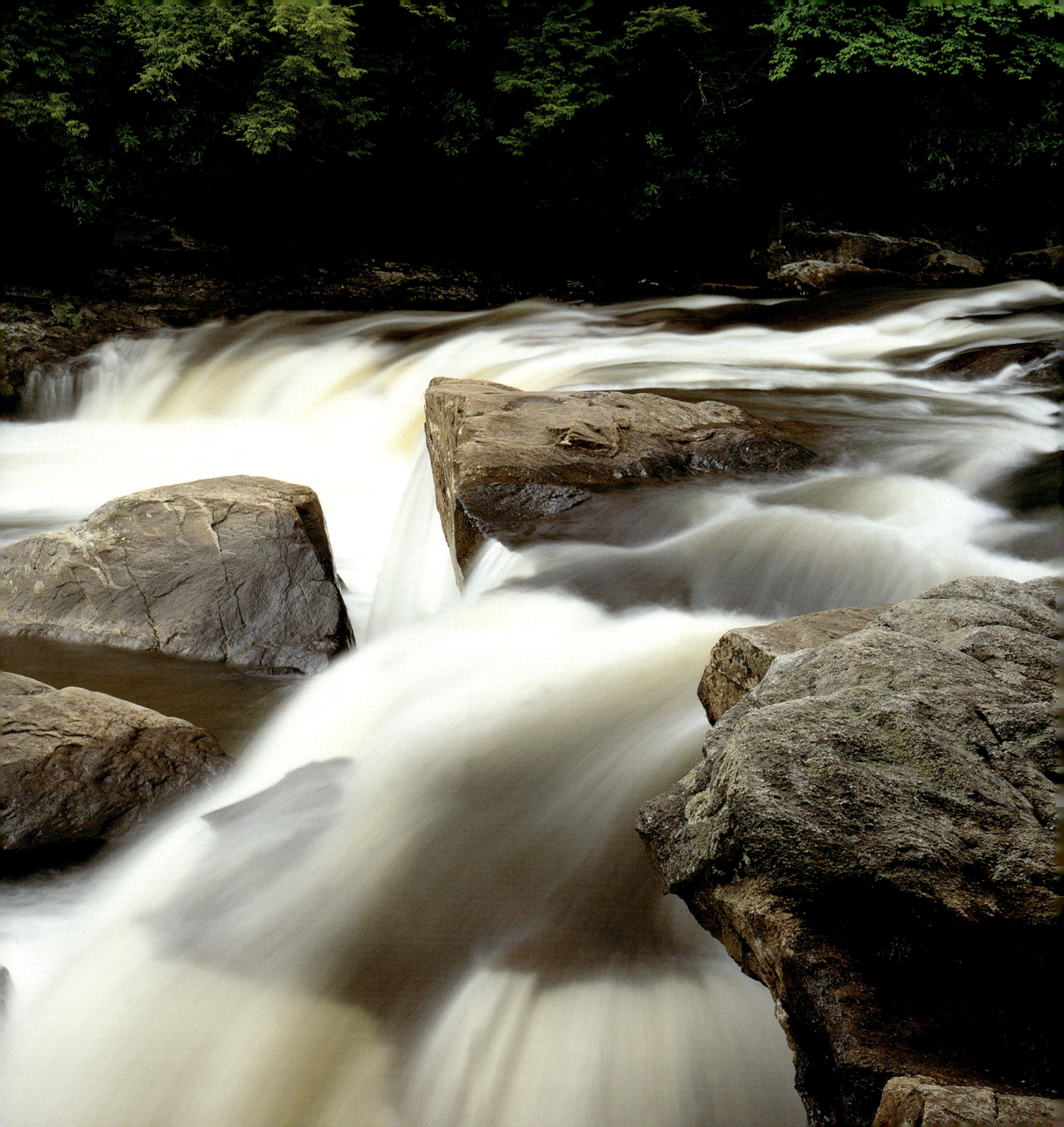

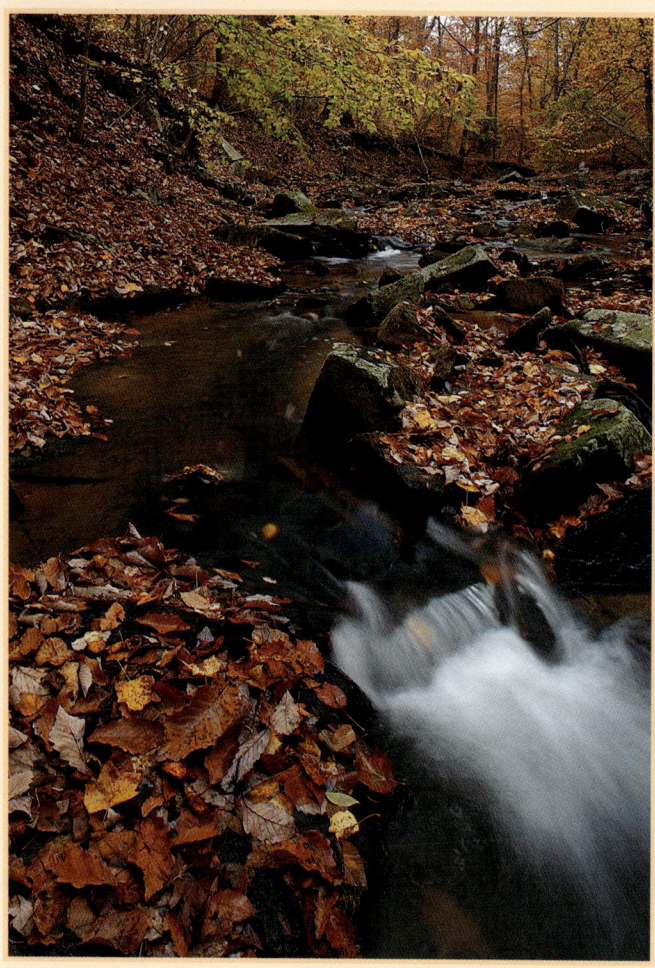

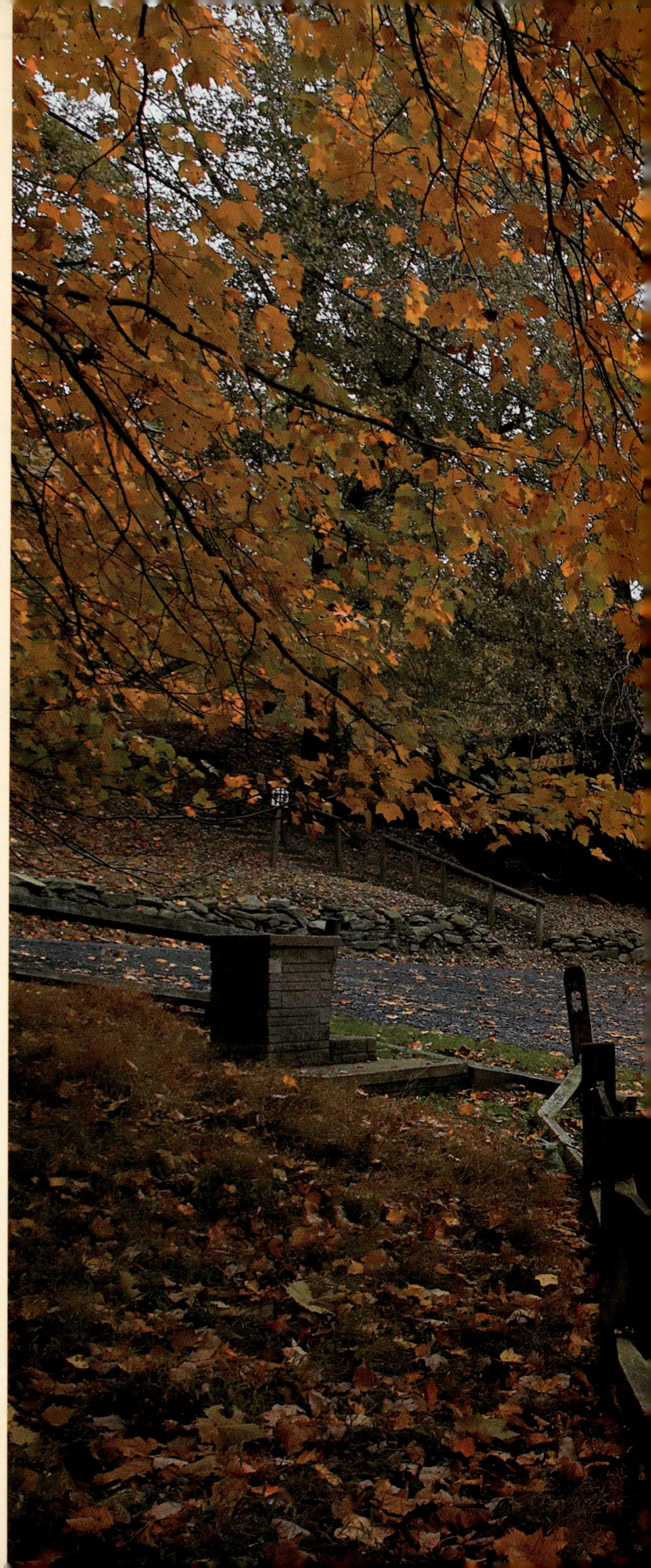

HISTORIC ROCK RUN Grist Mill, erected in 1794 by prosperous businessman John Stump, is a three story stone structure and is fully operational. The Mill sits on the shores of the lower Susquehanna River, several miles upstream of the Chesapeake Bay, in Susquehanna State Park.

Above: Rock Run in autumn.

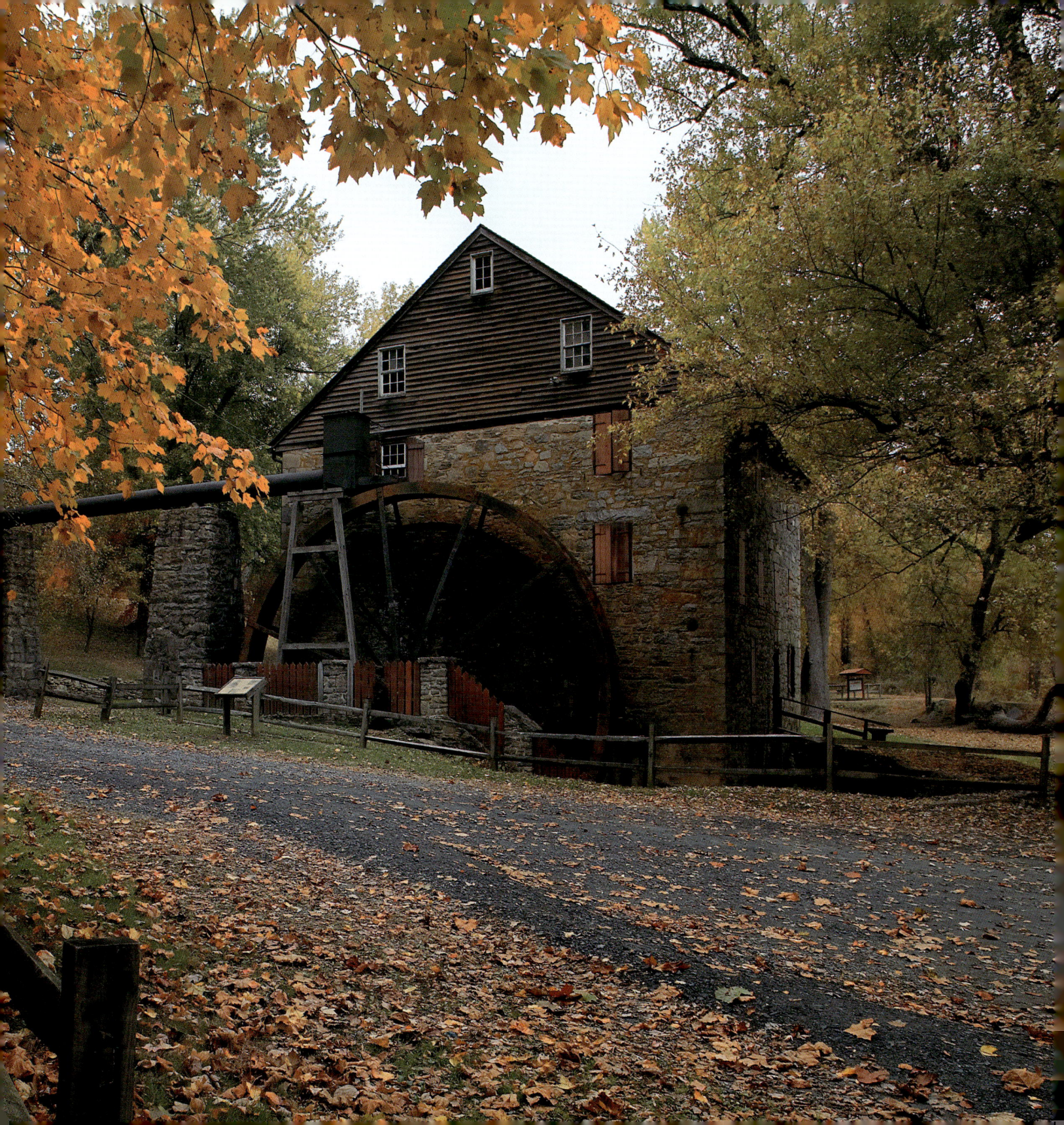

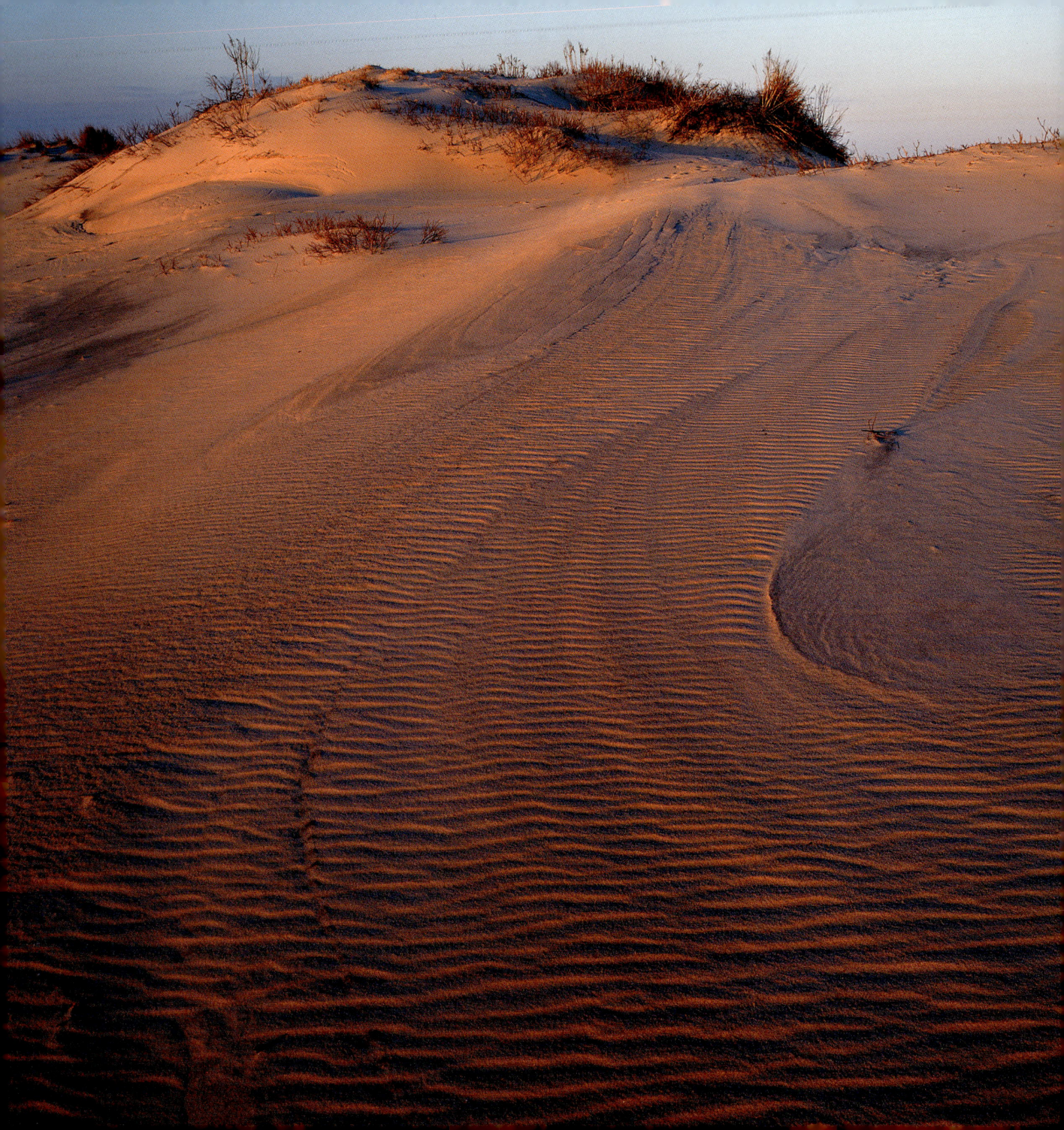

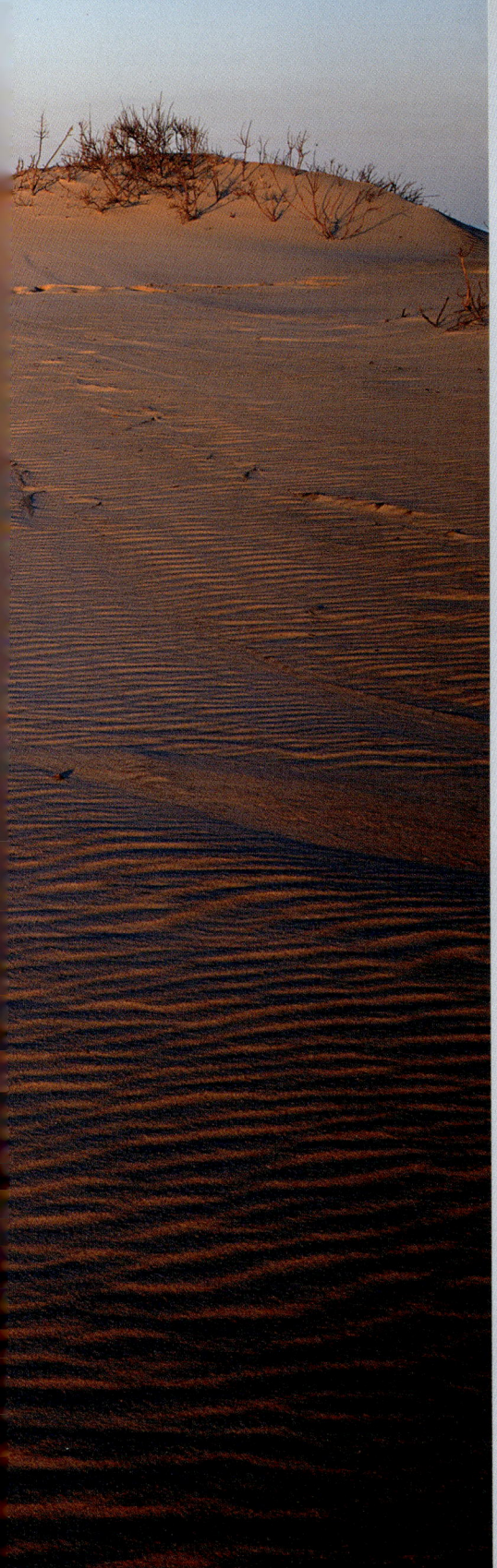

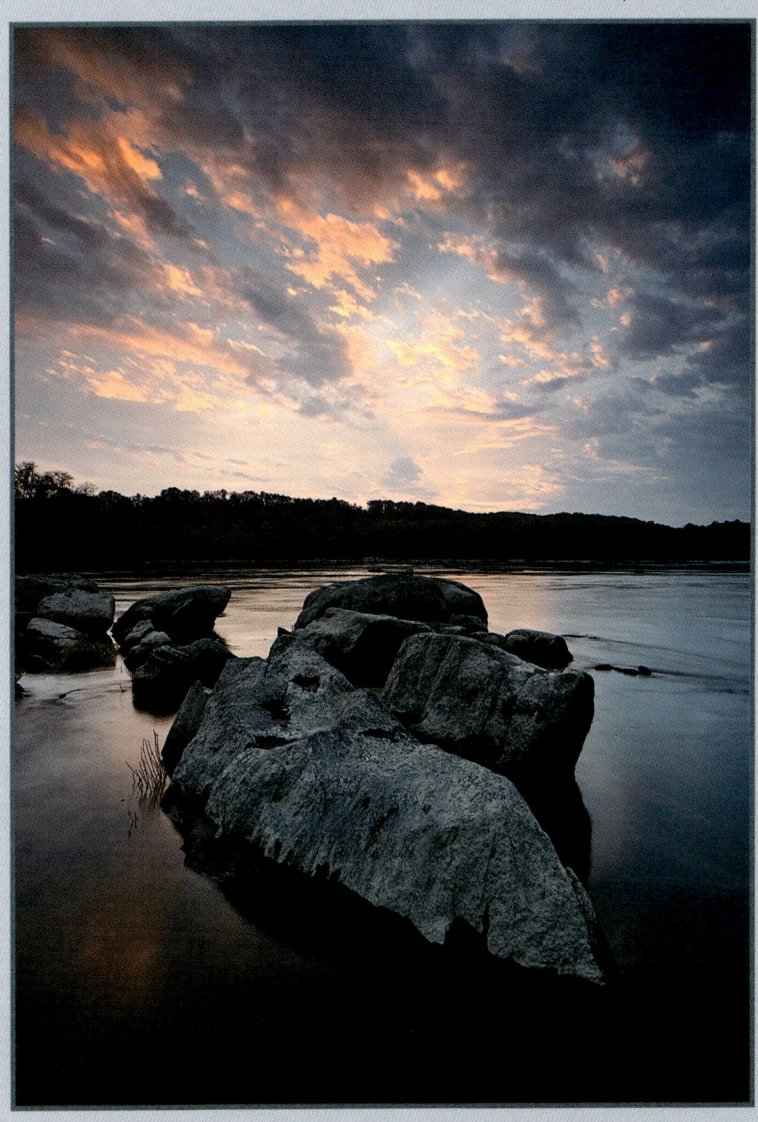

Left: A rippled dune catches evening light on Assateague Island.

Above: Rocks emerge from the tranquil waters of the Susquehanna River, Susquehanna State Park.

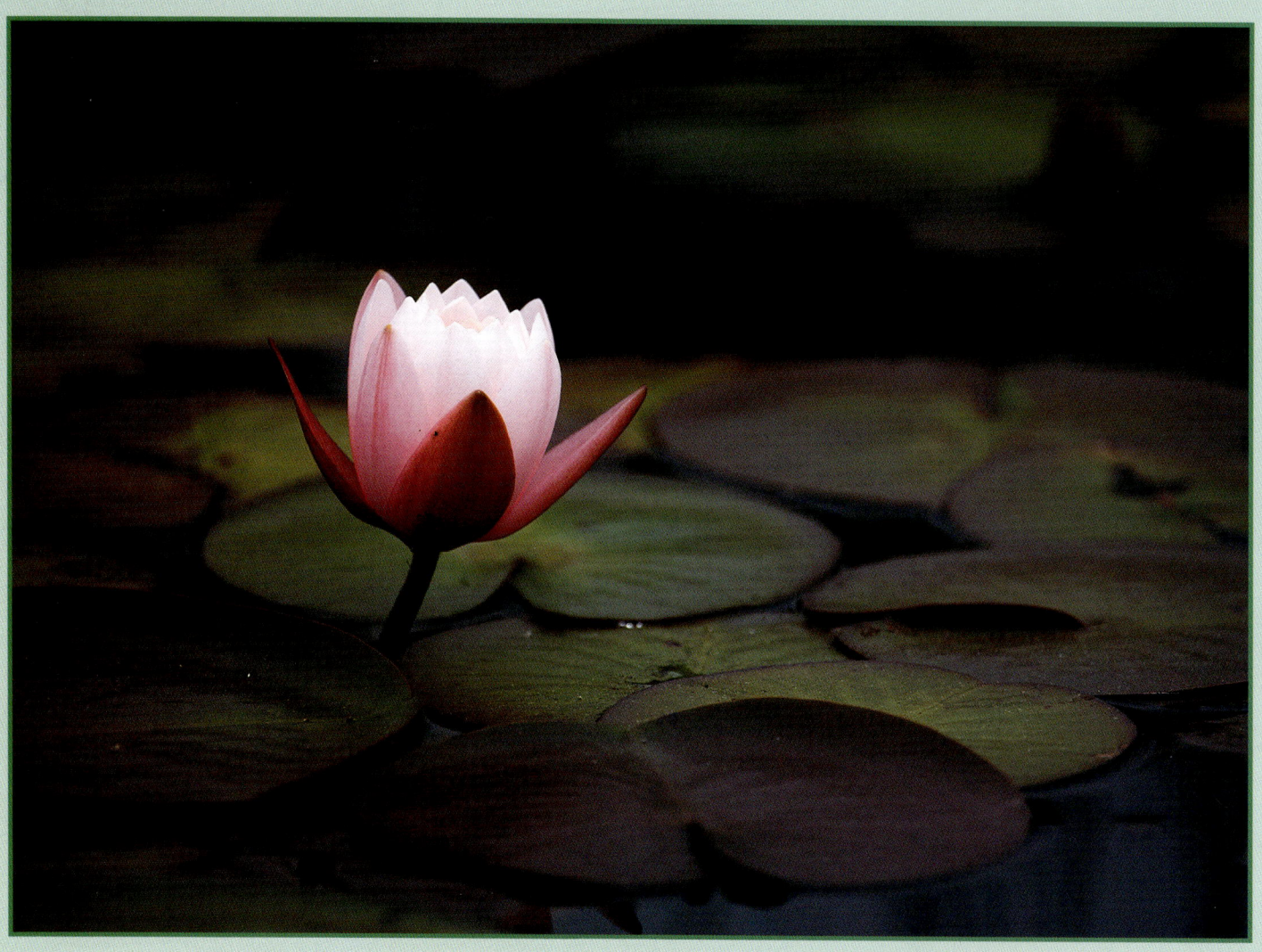

A water lily blossom emerges in spring in
Somerset County on Maryland's Eastern Shore.

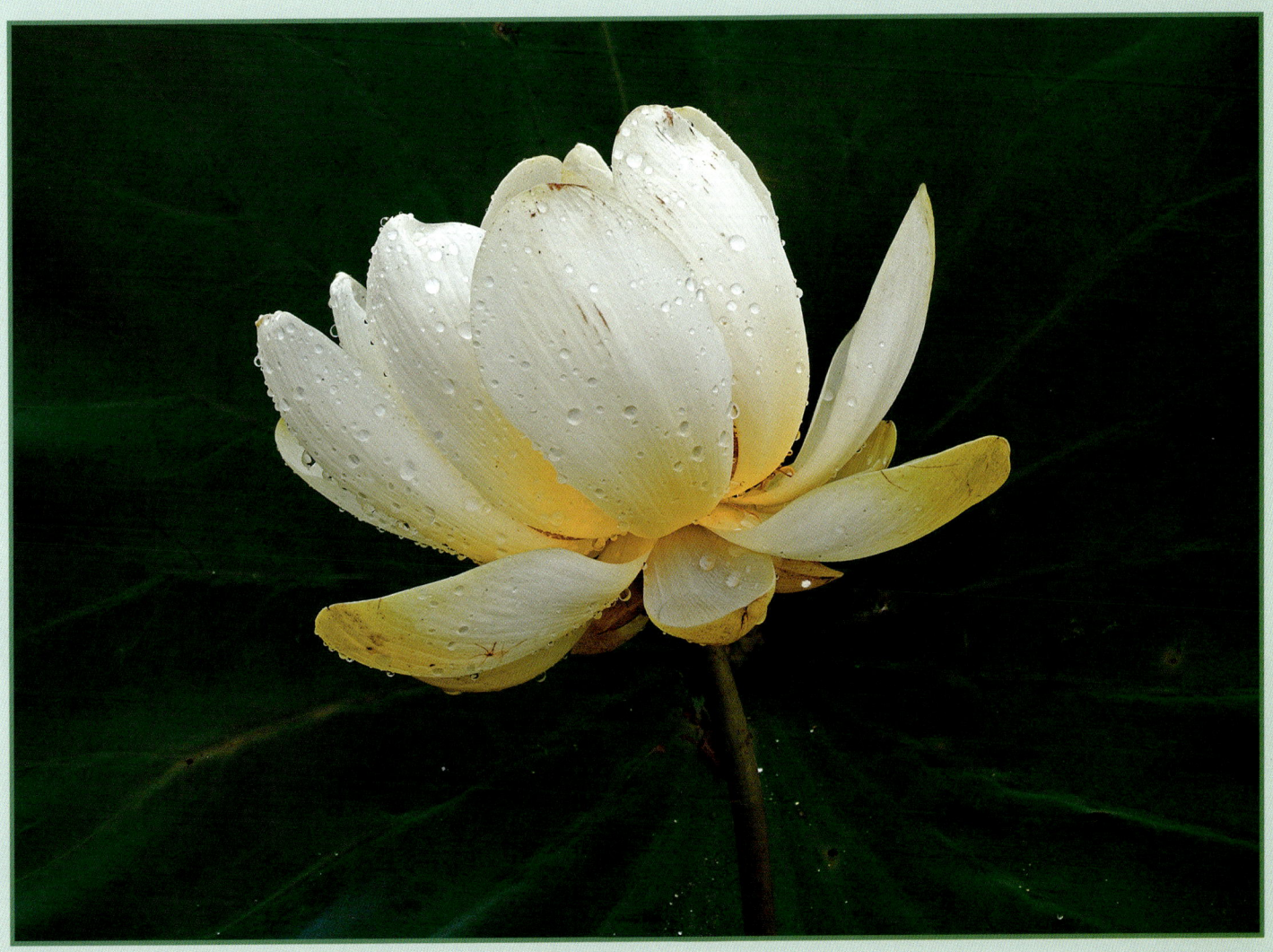

American lotus blooms in late summer
along Maryland's tidal waterways.

Next page: Dawn twilight over Cove Point Lighthouse,
on the Western Shore of the Chesapeake Bay.

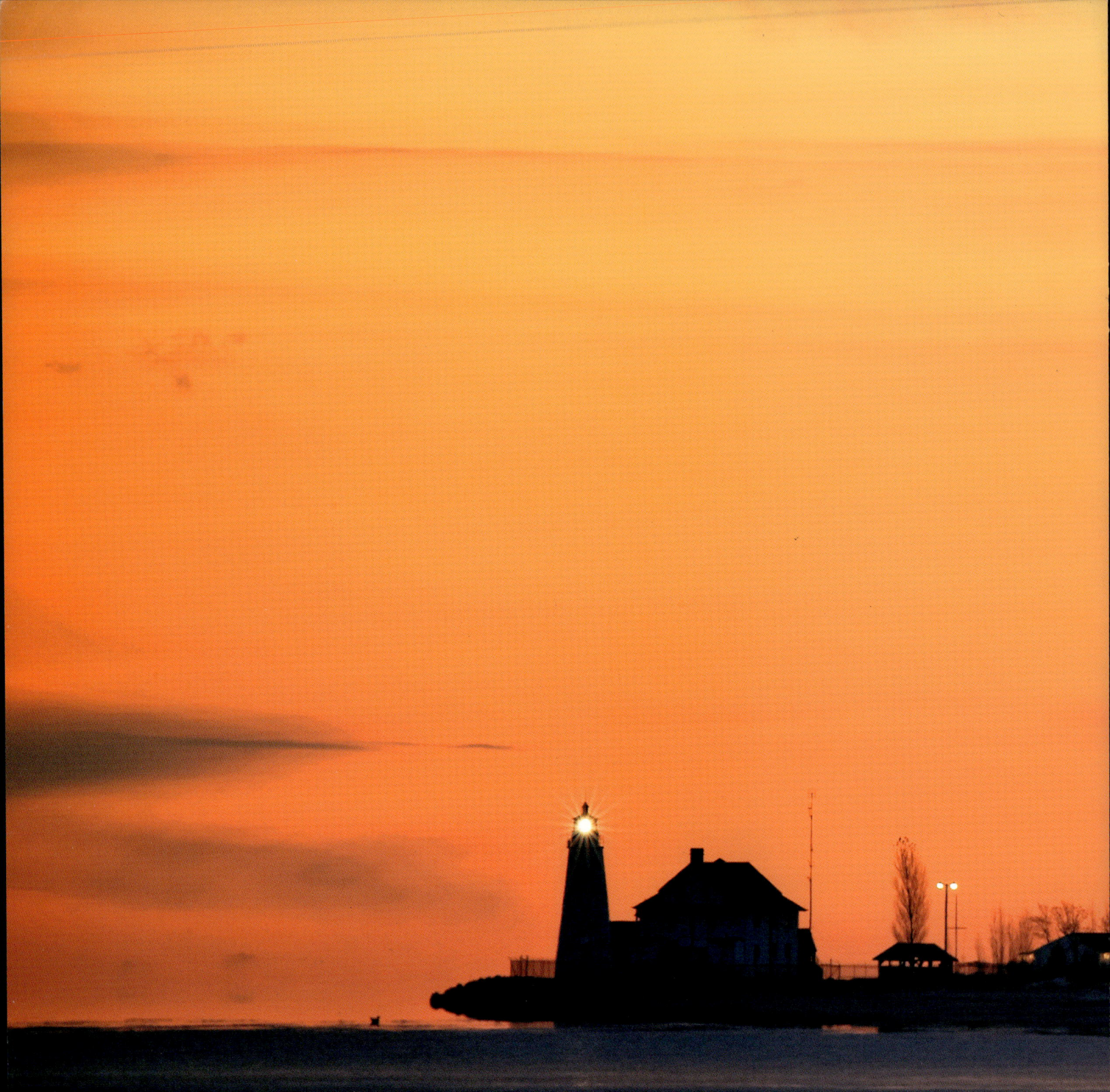

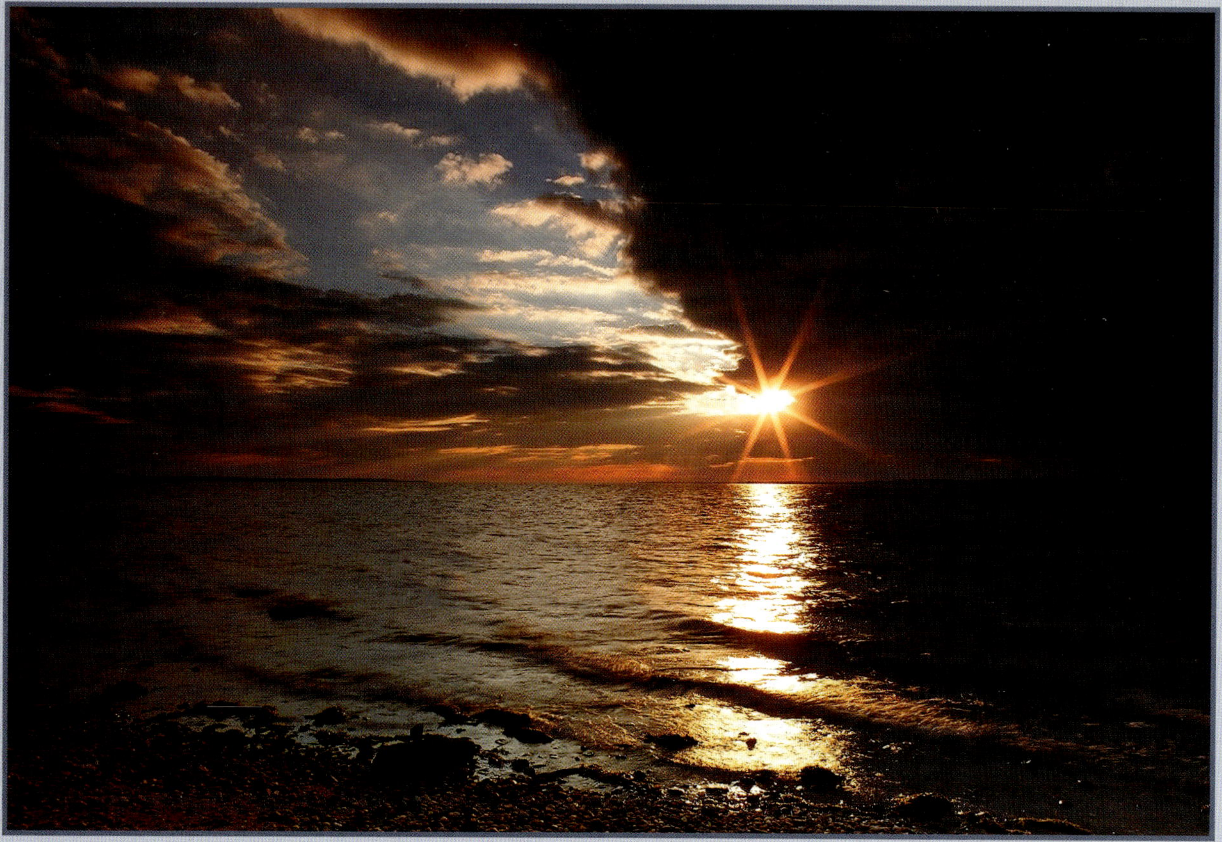

Above: Sunset over the Chesapeake Bay, Elk Neck State Park.

Back cover: Autumn hillside above Deep Creek Lake, Garrett County.

About the Photographer: Ian J. Plant has been photographing our natural world for the past ten years. His work has appeared in a number of books and magazines. Ian lives in Lorton, Virginia with his wife Kristin and their cats Kali and Stinky Pete.

Other books featuring images by Ian J. Plant:
Shenandoah Wonder and Light
Virginia Wonder and Light
Blue Ridge Parkway Wonder and Light
West Virginia Wonder and Light

www.ipphotography.com
You can see more of Ian's work on his website, www.ipphotography.com. There you can make on-line purchases of fine art prints of many of the images featured in this book, as well as other images from around the country.

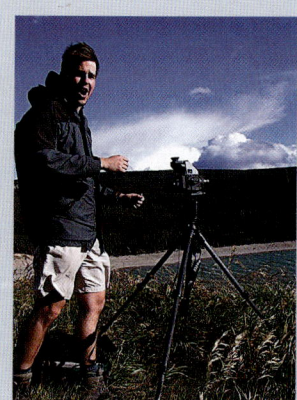